PLEASE ALL RISE!

A PLEA FOR A RAISE IN CONSCIOUSNESS

OSCAR J. FRYE

Copyright © 2022 by Oscar J. Frye

All rights reserved. No part of this publication may be reproduced, stored or transmitted in any form or by any means, electronic, mechanical, photocopying, recording, scanning, or otherwise without written permission from the publisher. It is illegal to copy this book, post it to a website, or distribute it by any other means without permission.

First edition

I pray and write for a better world,
for your children, and mine.
To Miguel, Luiza, Carlos and Teresa.

CONTENTS

Introduction 6

1. Are you happy like this, or is something still missing? 9
2. Cultivate your spirituality next to pursuing material objectives. 14
3. Why are you here? 19
4. What is the meaning of our life? 24
5. How to deal with aging? 28
6. How to see our time passing? 31
7. Your life, the cycles in nature, and reincarnation. 35
8. Your life, your existence and reincarnation. 37
9. The hidden gift behind our sacrifices, struggles, and suffering. 40
10. How to deal with a crisis? 43
11. Unlearning the habit of comparing ourselves to others. 49
12. You are unique, you are the hero of your life. 53
13. Building one's spiritual understanding. 58
14. Collective consciousness: The state of the world 62
15. Our successes and failures seen in the light of our spiritual evolution. 65

16. How not to judge and label at once every event in our life? 68

17. How to raise society's level of consciousness? 72

18. Connecting to the internet and connecting to the Divine. 75

19. How do many of us see our fellow man? 78

20. We are all busy, but are we busy doing the right things? 81

21. Be your own spiritual coach: In calmness, turn inward, and trust yourself. 88

22. Be your own spiritual coach: Open-up to discover your spiritual self. 91

23. Be your own spiritual coach: Turn your inner voice into a precious ally. 95

24. Be your own spiritual coach: Spend your precious time wisely. 101

25. Be your own spiritual coach: Bring positive energy, create beauty and change the world. 103

26. How to start up your spiritual practice? 106

27. Considerations to take along on the spiritual path. 115

Introduction

The current state of the world begs us to realize that we are on the wrong track, as the world population. We need a collective wake-up call.

I try to raise people's level of consciousness by encouraging them to stand still and look in the mirror and question their ways. The first thing we could re-discover when we look in the mirror, is that we are not what we see, we are inside of what we see.

We must learn to see through our physical envelope and realize our true nature is soul, before anything else. From the moment you realize this, you will understand that focusing on material things in life, might get you comfortable conditions in the here and now, but unless you also take care of your soul needs, you will have difficulty reaching greater satisfaction and true fulfillment in your life, and risk progressing less, or not at all, in your spiritual evolution.

Earthly life will never be completely fulfilling or perfect, because it simply isn't meant to serve such a purpose. Life on earth is not intended to be a dream vacation but rather a workplace, and people generally come back one life after another, to resume each time their unfinished business.

While on earth, man has higher objectives to pursue than all the material things this world can offer. As children of God, of the creator, of the universe, or whatever you want to call it, we must spiritualize our lives. We are all loving and caring beings at our core, but we can't help wondering when looking at our world: How far have we gone astray as mankind?

Introduction

In today's life for example, we try to buy our way into happiness in our consumption-oriented society, only many never get there. The 'happy' few that do get there, experience at best a periodic high thanks to their latest acquisition. We postpone our happiness until the purchase of our next trophy. However great the thrill of buying new things can be, it can't be confounded with true lasting happiness, which can only be reached by doing the right things, and there is no shortcut.

The focus of this book is always on the practical side of spirituality; everything is designed for a broad 'audience,' both subjects and writing style are accessible and inclusive to all.

The chapter headings listed in the contents bring immediate identification because all subjects deal with day-to-day life situations.

We cannot change people, but we can better ourselves, and so, serve as positive role models. When we become gentler, kinder and more patient, we bring positive energy into our environment, and that positive energy will always come back to us, uplifting us, helping us.

I encourage people to use their precious time wisely, and to learn to reframe difficult and challenging life events and see them as spiritual stepping stones, learning lessons and challenges that needed to be faced.

Constructing meaning in this manner is a noble effort from a spiritual point of view, because one recognizes the influence of both worlds we live in; the visible and the invisible –and this doesn't come easy as we are more inclined to tell ourselves it's all 'bad luck'. When we succeed in extracting sense out of hardship, we move closer to acceptance and so, we calm the storm inside.

When we learn to integrate the physical with the spiritual point of view in life, our efforts will be rewarded with ever-increasing understanding of life and beyond. We also realize that succeeding our earthly life is a must if you are keen on bringing home (into the afterlife) the fruits of your labor. Succeeding one's life spiritually, is essential to your evolutionary journey as a soul. This realization can 'save' one's life, 'setting you straight.'

When we realize we are souls, it follows that our souls need nourishment too. If our earthly dealings show no effort for spiritual growth, your soul could become disappointed with all the missed opportunities. No spiritual growth in a lifetime translates in a life that had not needed to be lived.

In the end there are 5 chapters on how to be your own spiritual coach. Give the 'mike' to your inner voice and see how refreshing a conversation you can have when he or she speaks out and quite surprisingly, turns into an insightful ally!

The before last chapter offers you 16 suggestions for your spiritual practice, and the last chapter contains thoughts and suggestions on how we could see the job of our life.

1. Are you happy like this, or is something still missing?

We are all observers in our life on this planet and sometimes, some of us might be willing to share a few of our observations to see if what we think or feel resonates with others, or if it's nothing more than the thought of one individual.

In our life, do we not say to ourselves from time to time, "Gee, if only I had this or that, or if only I could do this or be that, then I would be happy"?

It's that longing for certain things to materialize in our life I'm pointing at. I reckon most people have wants and desires; they build our motivation, it's what we work for, it's why we get up in the morning.

Most probably, in many a person's vision of their life, there's something missing or at least not yet completely satisfying. This is only logical given the long list of wants and needs that people typically have in our modern life.

When we compare ourselves to others, we often pick out those people who have something that we don't and would like to have too. We are drawn to what we don't have and nurture this feeling that something is lacking in our life instead of being more conscious of what we do have.

Why have we come to function like this? One reason might be that society tells us that it's good to always want more, to strive for more, to fight for better conditions, to work hard, and improve things. Yet hard work is no guarantee for a happier life, while it does take away most of our time.

Always wanting more. It's a noble quest, or that's what we say. In America, we even call it the American Dream, and we believe that we can make that dream come true with our own hands, through our sweat and tears.

Building steadily on small successes, patiently, one after the other, and thus, building our life, raising our comfort level. Many of us aim for this, climbing up the corporate ladder and rising to the top.

Many however, lag behind in this race to improve one's spending power and acquire better conditions. What can you do to improve your situation? You can choose to work harder or try to improve your skills and boost your market value.

Some people wonder if they need to change their selves or their behavior or anything that can help them become more effective and, hopefully, more successful.

Some turn to a coach to teach them how to improve their game, become fully aware of their strengths and how best to take advantage of them and improve their weak points.

In this way, we hope to come out stronger in the social arena and bring out the go-getter in us, the one that doesn't give up, the achiever.

Of course, it is fair to generally assume that self-empowerment and self-improvement will lead to better results, to more success, and thereby to more satisfaction in our professional life.

1. Are you happy like this, or is something still missing?

But still, I doubt most people will adopt and execute a self-improving action-plan because, in any busy adult's life, it isn't easy to find the time, energy, and money to start self-change and see it through until you have concrete results.

Thus, we postpone being happy because we're never quite ready, there is always something missing. When we believe, with the help of society, that our problems are of material nature, then we tend to focus on a material solution.

Along this line, we end up having people whose situations haven't changed over time and they tell themselves that they simply had no luck. Others realize that they could and/or should have put in greater effort to acquire more to be happier. Still, others who have done more and found more success have a more comfortable life. However, their improved situation simply took them to a higher level of spending, by merely upgrading their wishes and desires, keeping the same mechanism in place.

The root of the problem is that we often link our happiness to spending power, to how much money we have. The commercial world we live in does its best to reinforce this idea for us.

When we focus on what's missing of material nature in our life compared to others, we might even suffer from feelings of inferiority or experience frustration or jealousy, and as a result, fall even deeper into the system of working harder and harder to have more.

There are also examples of individuals that sail skillfully and successfully through life without experiencing too much stress while enjoying satisfying material conditions. My point, however, is to make a rough sketch of the most common problems people generally deal with.

All of this boils down to the concept of life we have and the analysis we make of our own situation. We must come to grips with the fact that modern society has many clear advantages, but some things might remain better the traditional way.

We have to be aware of modern-day society's influences on us and ask ourselves if they are wanted or not. It's a question of state of mind, or more exactly, the way we let ourselves be, the way we became over time, sculpted, conditioned by the world around us. We have picked up well all the wants and needs we think are our own, but are they really?

We could rethink our way of life and ask ourselves if we should not undo certain things, unload certain things we carry with us, and cut loose the unnecessary weight that strains our mental system and burdens us physically day in and day out.

There is so much unnecessary suffering because we took some wrong turns. We must see that all we do to try to make ourselves happier isn't also making us happier. We must try to get back on the right track.

When we travel through life with wants and desires that are not our own but stem from society and/or specific situations with the people that make up our life, our play, our theater, then we must ask ourselves if they have not become counterproductive.

If they have, they can start to blur the clarity that you need to keep a clear view of things, and so, only add confusion and take your mind off the essential issues. We spend so much precious time and energy focusing on material comfort, while we allocate so little time and effort to subjects and practices that can take us beyond the impermanence of our earthly theater.

1. Are you happy like this, or is something still missing?

We must try to think straight and look the facts in the eye. Material conditions should remain of peripheral importance and not become the main event or the core focus of anybody's life because, in itself, it's a meaningless achievement. Don't get me wrong, there is nothing wrong with money. It is the energy behind matter that transforms it into beauty or into something else.

If you happen to be rich, you better make sure you can show what beauty you created for a larger group than yourselves. If not, your precious money might transform into a weight, into a liability, over time. Don't count on blessings from above when you want money just to have money. Rather, cultivate a beautiful project in your mind where the interests of the greater group are central. Then you will have them interested!

2. Cultivate your spirituality next to pursuing material objectives.

The downside of our material society is that we didn't realize before starting the pursuit of happiness through material things, that this type of pursuit comes at a price.

When you set your mind on something, you "bathe" yourself in that mindset for as long as your mind is thus set. This conditions you; it shapes you on the inside in terms of what you identify with. It is important for us to think twice before we identify ourselves with something completely.

If your mindset is too focused on the material, it blinds you to other, more natural, and essential ways of being. You become disconnected from experiencing and growing in life, especially when you realize that you are a soul and, only temporarily, a human being.

Fully realizing this basic reality is what is needed. It is like the "ground zero" where you can then begin to build something substantial.

The way we spend our time tells us what we give priority to in our life. When you have more of one thing, you might have less of something else. More money, less time, more business meetings, less time for friends, and so on.

Time is the most precious asset we have in our life, so we better spend it wisely.

2. Cultivate your spirituality next to pursuing material objectives.

Instead of chasing material objectives, we could ask ourselves what we want to do with our life, what kind of person we want to be or become, what we stand for, what principles we uphold, and how we aim to contribute to making this world a better place.

Don't forget that when you have finished your education and start working and focus primarily on the money, you put your soul to sleep. When there is nothing interesting in the 'picture', your soul will be annoyed.

Picture your soul sitting in the back of the 'bus,' patiently watching how you manage your show on the road, and might find that you are not here to live a life with too much focus on material comfort. It is only when we turn our attention inward or wonder about what and who we are that we can start to understand what we are all about. From that moment on, real needs and desires can manifest.

As long as we keep believing that something is missing in our life, we are led to believe that the neighbor's grass is greener than our own.

But if you were to stand in your neighbor's garden, the grass would seem somewhat bleaker because we all have comparable problems to deal with; we just don't deal with them at the same time.

Comparing with others is a sure road to frustration, we should rather try to think straight and ask ourselves the right questions and then, apply some discipline to our conclusions.

If you think that material wealth can do the trick of making you happy, you may be thinking superficially. I believe that if you would meditate on the question, any sound human being, animated by a soul, reincarnating time and time again to continue to evolve spiritually, would most likely not direct all his or her time, energy, and attention to material affairs.

The evolved human being knows that our true identity is a reflection of the quality of the person we are, of what we think, of what we say, and of what we do for other people all throughout our life. Putting yourself in the place of someone else will transform you and make you more beautiful.

An evolved person will generally display personal qualities like patience, compassion, gentleness, kindness, even-mindedness, and so on, and be focused on understanding life, contributing to society, enhancing spiritual wisdom, and foremost demonstrating a great capacity to love.

We often lose sight of this and focus mainly on our temporary role in this life; our job. In a social setting, someone might well introduce himself, "Hi, I'm Steve. I'm a dentist." In truth, it should be, "Hi, people call me Steve here. I work as a dentist for the time being."

We must see that our job is only a part of what we are, or better, what we play, a role we take on for some time but that we can change. You can be a musician, then become a painter, or a teacher, or start to sell bicycles.

For any person having a temporary job while on earth, it is not easy to be completely happy because we are immeasurably more than our job title and all the things we do while working. We are not merely physical beings, and we can't expect ourselves to just be happy when we function on a predominantly superficial level.

This is sometimes the reason why people do volunteer work in their spare time, to add meaning to their life. You go home without getting

2. Cultivate your spirituality next to pursuing material objectives.

paid, but you feel great that you helped people and that they thanked you for it. It's a different trade-off.

I have no doubt that there are many rich but frustrated businessmen, disappointed in the power of their success. Some of them could be disappointed that the general feeling of success didn't flow through to their entire inner being nor to all aspects of their external lives.

They discover that the thrill of material success doesn't last forever and soon find that something in their lives is missing again. This might be the moment when some wake up and start to do more "good."

Well-equipped as they often are, with all the qualities they have cultivated throughout their lives, these people can indeed accomplish great things when they put their minds and their means to it.

Money is not that final destination you must absolutely get to, nor is it the magical cure for all one's difficulties in life. Money isn't right or wrong, but a neutral energy. It is not an objective to which one must direct all one's precious time, efforts, qualities, and abilities.

You can be successful and rich yet still experience unfulfillment if you had neglected your spiritual needs as an incarnated soul. The divine design predisposes us in such a way that true fulfillment cannot be attained through material things.

Today it seems that many of us have come to believe that the outside, material world can cater to practically all our needs. If this is our belief, we fail to consider that our very essence, our soul nature, needs nourishment too. Instead of turning to the outside world, we should simply turn inside and search there.

How do you turn inside? Unless you have already devoted time to spiritual practice next to your professional life, you must start developing new skills, such as being calm, listening to yourself, and developing your intuition.

When you decide to make an effort to bring yourself closer to your soul by stilling your body and taming your restless mind, you will soon realize that you're on the right track, because it feels like the most natural thing to do.

Compare it to learning to still oneself when out in nature to become one with it. When you succeed in becoming one, you see all at once that what appeared lifeless around you at first sight, is actually full of life.

Dead tree trunks seemed just dead tree trunks, until you zoomed in and saw that blanket of thick moist moss covering it, sheltering a variety of insects.

In nature, when you observe carefully, life will manifest. Within yourself, the same principle applies. When you're still and patient, "energies" will manifest. Please try and see for yourself.

3. Why are you here?

Do you ever think about why you are here?

It seems every person must discover the reason for being on this planet and ask him or herself if our earthly life has a function, a goal, an objective. Why are we here?

Unfortunately, I doubt if most people even consider the question. It seems almost as if we don't want to stand still and look at our lives more profoundly.

When we do take time to think about more profound topics, then often it's only for a moment, before we move back again to our daily business. In our Western world, we rather keep busy and keep moving because when we're moving all the time, like busy bees, we tell ourselves we're productive.

We happily show other people how busy we are and how hard we work as to merit their respect. But, seen from a spiritual point of view, even when we are terribly busy, although we might be accomplishing things on a material level, if our actions do not contribute something beneficial to a larger group, we are stuck on a superficial level, simply trying to render our own lives more comfortable.

It would be great if one could balance one's personal interests with contributing to other people's well-being. A medical doctor nicely balances both, because he has to continuously go out of his way to attend to his patients, but receives payment in return.

It is important that we stretch our consciousness, that we think about other people and include them in our projects. Every day that passes without any attention invested in raising our consciousness is a lost opportunity for spiritual growth.

I understand that many of us resist contemplating and discussing spiritual subjects. Perhaps the sheer vastness of that unknown dimension makes it an uncomfortable topic of discussion. Unless we educate ourselves, we can't know what to make of it. Fear of the unknown will only diminish as one approaches "the beast."

But of course, we feel better going through our daily routine where we are on top of things. The unseen world; we would rather not be confronted with it, so what do some of us do? We create a defense mechanism.

This defense mechanism is like putting up a mental wall around us. This wall keeps us "safe" from ideas that intend to reach us but that we would rather not look in the eye. In this way, we are only exposed to the more neutral stuff, the things we already know how to handle.

You can think of this mental barrier that we put up as being like a fence we put around cattle. Being fenced in, the world becomes smaller, and soon, one will look no more beyond the boundaries of that fence.

While the reality of the outside world remains unchanged, your mind becomes conditioned by that fence and will limit itself to that microenvironment, micro reality, that it seeks to expand no more, and actually retracts.

When we are fenced in and only have eyes for what's near, touchable and familiar, sadly enough, we take the wonder and the mystery out of

3. Why are you here?

our life, and speculate too little about stars, planets, and faraway galaxies, that meanwhile continue to exist the same way.

We must be aware of how our thinking patterns us, conditions us, predisposes us, and shapes our future. We shouldn't tie down our beautiful limitless human potential, and concern ourselves only with earthly matters, because we are intended to do the exactly the opposite; to make the fullest use of our capacities to advance on our journey of spiritual evolution.

The problem with betting on worldly things to bring you happiness is that their value is only relative, that is, their value is only what it means to you in the here and now, because at the end of your life you will leave all of it behind and continue your travels without it.

But all time, effort, and energy invested in something that raises your consciousness, instantly merges with your soul identity. This is really what and who you are, and it is what will accompany you into eternity. Please think about that, especially if you believe that your soul will exist beyond this life.

As a matter of fact, it's only natural to develop one's interest in the spiritual realm because you are, first of all, a soul.

On the other hand, I can understand that because we have unfamiliarized ourselves with the unknown world or dimension, we feel somewhat uneasy discussing this. Even so, it remains the place where we come from and where we will return. No one can change or escape that reality.

That's why we have an innate longing for spiritual practice. People that discover this dimension in their life and dedicate time to practice soon find that they can't live without it anymore. They feel and know pertinently that their action touches the heart of what's essential in their life.

On a deeper level, we are all inclined and capable of embracing our soul dimension effortlessly and harmoniously. As human beings, we have at our disposal all the necessary qualities to cultivate our awareness of our true soul essence.

Our soul is longing for us to tap into that innate quality we all have to connect with it, and so, succeed in finding that balance in our life between all our worldly business and the higher dimension.

There is nothing really extraordinary about connecting with the above, or with the universe. Many peoples the world over (native American Indians, for example) live connected with nature and the spirit world, made manifest by numerous rituals and offerings. It is inherently part of their experience of life.

These tribes show us their example of interacting respectfully with nature, ensuring a durable co-existence with it. In contrast, the more evolved cultures or industrialized nations focused on taking from nature, to the extent of depleting the earth's resources and destabilizing the global ecosystem.

These tribes are routinely still referred to as primitive cultures, because they have less of what we so identify with, what we value so much, that is material things.

A simpler life in form perhaps, but a more balanced attitude towards nature and a more sophisticated life in a spiritual sense, because they never turned their back on the higher forces.

3. Why are you here?

The unseen or spirit world remained an integral part of their setting, their culture, and their natural environment. Despite their primitive ways, the spirit world around them was not denied, it was acknowledged, it was respected, and it was worshipped...and they were right.

We have lost our connection with the universe, because we have downgraded our understanding of life. We lowered our vision of life to a practical, material, down-to-earth kind of concept, where the spiritual and higher dimension are systematically neglected.

We tell ourselves that our modern society is superior, and more evolved than primitive cultures, but before discarding all such tradition, we could have thought twice.

If some elements could have been kept alive through some form of practice in our modern societies, then we wouldn't have drifted off so far, away from this connection, and we wouldn't have to make a U-turn to retrieve it.

On the other side, when you do take just a little time to open yourself to some kind of spiritual practice, it could feel like intuitively finding your way back home in the dark.

Good luck to you all.

4. What is the meaning of our life?

As mentioned, I feel that we should carefully think about what we do with our time. What we do with our time reveals the concept we hold of life.

We can see ourselves merely as human beings with a physical body and a brain, trying to lead as happy a life as possible, or give further meaning to our life, to ourselves, by realizing or believing that we have a soul nature.

If you believe that you have a soul, and you like the idea of putting some time and effort into spiritual thought, discussion, and practice, then the next thing you must decide is how much time you actually want to put into it.

If you look at your life and say you only have little time to offer, then you will most probably advance only modestly as most people do. But, if we would all observe our world and see the destructive forces at work, as well as the way we are treating mother nature, we are likely to get the sense of urgency and be inspired to come together to save humanity from its own dark side, and realize that a serious collective effort is needed.

So, in case you do want to make an effort, you have to know how to make the best use of your time. The answer could be to start investigating, reading, and thinking, to come to realize that we are here to raise our level of consciousness, and that we should evolve accordingly in our decisions and actions.

Why do we need to construct meaning?

4. What is the meaning of our life?

Because it's our foremost goal in life to construct meaning as soon as we can, to look around us, above us, and in the mirror, and see what we can make of it.

What's our place in all of this?

You can never start early enough because the more meaning you can construct, the more you will chase away the uneasiness or restlessness that somehow comes over us as we grow older and think about the time when our life will come to end.

The greatest goods one can acquire are immaterial and these often need to be cultivated. Love and wisdom are the key qualities one must nurture.

Love conquers all, and wisdom is the antidote against many forms of suffering. These are necessary attributes to have with you as you grow older. They allow you to put things in perspective, remain positive and keep your faith intact.

We want to avoid a feeling of failure once we pass over, of not having used our time wisely, of not having considered enough the most important subject of our lives, that is, the reason for us actually being here.

Just imagine leaving while knowing that you left so much unattended, undone, unresolved, and untouched. Once back with your soul mates, you might say to yourself, "I could have done more", and this might make you feel sorry, realizing that you lost a precious opportunity.

The purpose of my writing is only to contribute to a process of waking up or simply becoming aware of this reality. Whether or not you acknowledge this will not change the reality of it. It is your free will that allows you to attend to it or not, and that is precisely the way it is meant to be. It is all up to you.

When one does try to understand more, these efforts are likely to be compensated by a sense of greater meaning in one's life; meaning that nothing of earthly matter or pleasure can give you.

When engaged on this path, that sense of meaning might eventually become so great that you feel that it is the most wonderful thing you can do with your time. Naturally, it then becomes the driving force behind your life, and you realize from that day on, that it is the only subject that truly deserves your time and attention.

Now, if you're thinking about all of these then you're doing a great job already. You're on target, increasing your awareness, and fine-tuning your level of consciousness.

When you think deeply about things, sometimes you change your opinion. You may change your idea of something because you received new information. At times, you will replace a piece of your puzzle; the puzzle being your own personal world map, in essence, the way you see and experience things, your understanding of the world you're living in.

The construction of this world map is dynamic. As you find out more, you think about what to believe: that new piece of information or the one currently in place? If you want to change a piece, you deconstruct and then you reconstruct. This process will last your entire life, and beyond in the afterlife, and then again back on the planet.

You act on your findings and you adjust your world map, your puzzle accordingly, and your puzzle reflects what you are. What you hold up as

4. What is the meaning of our life?

true and important will direct your actions. Your thoughts, beliefs, and manners even, show what you are on the inside.

Since most of us can't stop thinking, this process continues all the time. In this way you shape and reshape yourself going along the way, year after year, all throughout your life. The purpose is to better yourself, to upgrade yourself to become your best or highest version. This is the constant process of man's spiritual evolution.

Remember, it's a slow process, depending on the complexity of the questions at hand. Replacing just one piece of your world map or puzzle, could take you years, decades, an entire lifetime, or even more. It all depends on your personal effort. You're free to determine your input, but don't forget that with choice comes responsibility.

The efforts you make will bring you increased awareness and higher consciousness. Postponing taking on the only real job of your life could make you feel sorry later when you realize you didn't give it your best shot because it wasn't your priority.

By raising our level of consciousness, we evolve in our decisions and actions, becoming less self-centered, more open, and aware of others' feelings, and so more responsible in a social sense.

With each thought and action, we shape, like a sculptor, our person, our being, making it more beautiful, more like it was meant to be, an extension on earth of our own universal soul.

In this manner, we grow in beauty as our contribution to other people, to society, takes form. Then what once was a little light, your light, will shine stronger and stronger... and so it was meant to be, so it will be, for each and every one of us, over time, at the rhythm of your own free will.

5. How to deal with aging?

This time I would like to touch upon something that we all know very well. At first, when we're young, we want it so much that it keeps us from sleeping at night. Over time, however, most of us change our minds, and for some, it turns into a bad dream. What could this be? Aging!

We have no choice other than to accept the aging process. We can strive to be as physically fit as possible to preserve our mobility and our independence, but we must at the same time not cling to an ideal of our physical body that is unrealistic, as not to lose ourselves in chasing perfection, something that can never be.

We should instead work on accepting this natural and gradual process of physical change that goes hand in hand with the time passing in our life.

Everything is dynamic in our life, ever-changing, in constant preparation for the next phase. We slowly move from young and beautiful to old and grey, almost as to already prepare us bit by bit, that one day, we will go back again. It's part of the divine design of our lives.

Also, pursuing perfection, in general, is like chasing a ghost; you'll never get it. Perfection is a land or a place where nobody has ever been. Even if you could go there, there wouldn't be much to do for us anyway because we need imperfection to fuel our actions.

An imperfect state keeps us on the move, working and trying. A perfect state of things would leave no room for improvement, making action unnecessary. Stopping the movement, and we would risk imploding. In

5. How to deal with aging?

life, I believe it is the process that counts, the growing, the learning, the sculpting of one's qualities, bit by bit, continuously over time.

When your life is perfect, all is easy, there's no challenge, you can't grow, and our life is about exactly the opposite. It is about what you can manifest when things are difficult and what beauty you can make from what you have 'in your hands'.

Trying to let your light shine through the dark clouds of trouble, pain, or hardship, is manifesting real power, a power or energy far more potent than the energy we have when striving to be physically perfect. We can't ever be perfect, only our actions can.

When we drift off course, pursuing perfection or living too superficially, we might need a wake-up call to set us straight. Wake-up calls come disguised in many forms, personal disaster, disease, accidents, hardship, difficulties, and so on.

Wake-up calls are meant to knock us out of our way, out of our daily routine and habitual ways, to bring us to a full and sudden stand still, to open our eyes, to make us think about what we are doing, with our time, with our life. This is the time to ask yourself if you have been making the right choices.

The probable realization that all wasn't exemplary, and the changes that you could subsequently make in your life, is the hidden gift one must learn to discover in times of trouble.

In retrospect, you will come to see more clearly why that challenge needed to happen in your life, needed to be presented to you, what it brought you, and what it taught you.

For the universal plan is not to break us, but to burden us to the extent of what we can handle. Unless we are challenged deeply, man is not inclined to self-reflection and even less to self-change.

Unless encouraged, many remain spiritually uninspired, and because spiritual progress is exactly what life is all about, we are put in difficult situations to make us think.

Once we have thought enough, it is up to ourselves, with our free will to decide if we want to do something about it, if we want to make a change in our life, or instead, if we prefer to prepare to defend our position when we pass over, that it was simply too difficult, too much to ask.

We can often see in ourselves what needs to be changed, but still, struggle with the execution of it. All people struggle with this, but perhaps you have the courage to try, and see if you can make a difference.

Let's see if you can bring out the hero in you. I wish you good luck.

6. How to see our time passing?

Besides having to deal with aging, we are also confronted with the ever-diminishing amount of time that we have left in our life.

I think most people believe that time passes too fast, but when we look at how we experience the passing of time, we can say it's pretty smart clockwork.

The pace at which our time ticks away is not a coincidence. It passes slowly enough to keep us from despair, thinking that the end of our life might be approaching, and yet it passes fast enough to make us understand that our time here on earth is precious and that we should spend it wisely.

Although many people understand that their time is precious, that understanding isn't always enough to motivate them to think deeply about their lives, about why they received the gift of life and what it implies.

What can we do to make us feel at peace with the idea, or the knowledge even, that our time is ticking away?

The fact that time passes as it does, can't be changed by us. What can we do? Well, if you can't beat them, join them, or here, don't go against it, go with it and accept it as a fact of life. Also, you can tell yourself that a force greater than you can imagine, created it, specifically to be like this, for you, and every other person on this planet.

The amount of time we have in each life, and the pace time ticks away, are part of the conditions on earth needed for our human experience. It makes up the scene, the theater, the set of our life, where all elements play their part in creating the illusion, in upholding the show that you must try to discern; to broaden ever further the scope of your understanding.

Even if you could stop time for yourself, would you? If you would, you would be the only one that wouldn't grow older? How comfortable would that be? I think we would all be wiser to trust the plan; the divine design.

Our lives are planned to be lived, in a specific period in time, and our birth takes place also at a precisely chosen place in time. Why?

To make sure that you encounter the best opportunities for personal growth and spiritual evolution, specific life situations are offered to you so that, at a specific moment in your life, you will encounter exactly that what you need to experience.

If these specific life situations couldn't be created, then it would mean leaving your entire life experience to chance, to coincidental happenings, to see once your life is over, if, by chance, your life turned out to be interesting, or perhaps not at all.

With time, everything changes. The quality of time itself also changes in our subjective perception as we grow older. Time often sheds a different light on events concerning "unfinished business" between people, because people change over time. For example, the passing of time sometimes takes off the rough edges.

6. How to see our time passing?

In this way, time enables people to revise their opinions and attitudes about things, hopefully helping to wash away the bitterness that sometimes stays after a conflict, a clash, or an unfortunate event.

Time also puts the same individual in different spots during his or her lifetime, according to life phases that change. Imagine, for example, a young boy who mattered to none grows into a big, strong, dominant man in his village. Then as the years tick away, the physical power he enjoyed for much of his adult life and banked on as a comparative advantage, slowly fades away as his body ages, becoming an older man.

Imagine all the psychological changes that accompany the aging process of this imaginary character and the impact they have on how he positions himself in the social arena. Even when your entire life is perfectly stable, dealing with the passage of time remains a challenging issue to handle even-mindedly.

Most lives are not that stable and are full of surprises or synchronicities, because unforeseen events bring about the changes that needed to take place in a life, often for the person to experience that what was part of the life-plan.

Although many situations are flexible and leave you to decide with your own free will, it seems that at least some key events or meetings in one's life are likely to stand as unavoidable, non-negotiable on your life's menu, simply because such events are the main reason why you came to this life.

The areas we must most often learn in, are love, forgiveness, patience, compassion, selflessness, to name but a few, and because these experiences are social in nature, they can only be had through the interaction with other people, or rather through the interaction with specific individuals.

Why? Because most of us have had many lives, and inevitably, karma, and karmic issues need to play out between the same people (souls) that created them. Since karmic accounts need to be balanced, specific life situations are created as an opportunity to even the debt.

You can be sure that the people you interact with in your life are not there by chance.

All the characters involved in a particular life situation must appear in the right place, at the right time, in the right form, and with the right mind-set. For all these elements to coincide, it suggests to me that there must be some kind of planning going on about at least some key issues in our life.

If there is no interference, no direction, no management from above, all interaction would be random or spontaneous, and most likely, nothing much would come of it other than the typical behaviors people demonstrate when left uninspired. I don't believe that, I rather have confidence in the intelligence of the universe and their invisible touch.

As with any experience that has a function, a goal, it is logical that your earthly life has a beginning and an end, and a review period afterward to see what sense you can make of your earthly life when you're up there, high in the sky, with all the time in the world to reflect about it.

7. Your life, the cycles in nature, and reincarnation.

In our life, we are used to the cycles we see in nature. We are used to summer as we are to winter. We get up in the morning with sunlight and go to sleep when the moon takes the place of the sun. We look for small seafood between the rocks with low tide and patiently wait to sail out of the harbor with the flow, and so on.

We can see how natural cycles pattern our lives. Our biological clock, our original setting, indicates that we function best when aligned with the natural flow of things, which proves that we are part of nature.

Wouldn't it be logical then, when we can say we are part of nature, that our lives are cyclical too, just like in nature? Over time, many seasons come and go, and many lives are lived. The thought appears perhaps less obvious to you because you can't see it happening before your own eyes, but that doesn't mean that it isn't so.

I believe that your soul continues to exist after death as consciousness and that, after some time, it takes on a new body for a new life. Our spiritual evolution on earth has a clear goal, that is, spiritual enlightenment, and this can't be reached in one lifetime. Therefore, we need to come back, and many times so.

I started to read a long time ago about reincarnation, not to say that I have read a lot about the subject. No, that wasn't necessary because I accepted it naturally. The greatest gift I received from embracing the idea of reincarnation is that everything became so much clearer almost at once.

We inherit from ourselves, from our own actions and our own doings, indeed we reap what we sow. This helps so much in explaining our own life as well as the lives of others and shows us the immortality of our souls.

Even if you believe in nothing, as long as you are a good person, you'll have nothing to worry about. To me, the point is not only what you believe but also how you explain it to yourself.

Even when you believe in nothing, you still see the stars at night, and then you also surely wonder sometimes what it is you are staring at.

If you want an explanation for the things you hear, see or wonder about, one has to investigate, and this principle will always apply in the here and now and in the hereafter.

When you investigate and find an explanation that suits your mind, you will be happy with it, because it helps you to build your understanding of the world you're living in.

Whereas, if you don't investigate, you will have to accept that you don't really know. Ask yourself if you are comfortable with that. I believe people have an innate longing for learning more about their spiritual nature.

At around twenty years of age, I was somewhat restless. I already thought time was passing fast but had no clear idea of what would happen at the end of my life—Whether or not somehow, something of myself would continue to exist after death.

I chose to investigate, and soon I was happy I did, finding out that our path of spiritual evolution is long and that we must live many lives.

Our life is about experience and growth. Nothing else can truly be obtained or lastingly kept. Nothing of material nature can be taken with you, but your life lessons will travel with you. They become part of what you are.

8. Your life, your existence and reincarnation.

This time I would like to put the idea of reincarnation, which is perhaps still a vague, strange, and exotic idea to you, in a more familiar context to try to make it clearer.

Imagine a very long passenger train composed of many wagons, riding steadily across lands that stretch endlessly ahead. See this long train as your existence, see each wagon as one life, and see the train moving along as time passing by.

You can't feel the train's speed, nor can you feel the time passing by in your own life. The lands that stretch endlessly ahead are like eternity that lays in front of you and the endless time your soul has to accomplish its spiritual evolution.

The driver of this train is an older, wise, kind, and patient man, and he maneuvers the train skillfully through the valleys and over the land to ensure that all goes as scheduled. The driver, who represents the universe, accompanies you all along your life journey, ensuring that all things that should happen, happen as planned before boarding.

Before you were born, you agreed to be put on this train, and in a specific wagon, but you cannot remember this. In the same way, you accepted your present life and its conditions before birth yet don't remember that either.

You don't realize that you are in a wagon or on a train, just like you do not realize that your current life represents only just a tiny portion of your total existence as a soul.

In your wagon, you are so absorbed by work, financial issues, emotional relationships, friendships, wanting and buying material things, and taking selfies, that you rarely think of anything out of the box, out of the wagon, anymore.

Again, this is much like your real life, where we are so absorbed by the illusion of material, temporary life that we hardly ever take a break and think about our existence.

Your travel companions in the wagon are like the people that make up your life; family, friends, colleagues, and strangers. Even strangers can be old friends, from other lives.

Over time, you discover you have affinity with some, and less with others, but the person you least like might become your cabinmate, and then perhaps, your best friend. In the end, your life is all about the love and other fine qualities that people can manifest towards each other.

Sometimes in the wagon somebody gets up, moves out of sight, and doesn't come back. This we also know in our life as death. A person leaves your wagon, and doesn't come back, and after some time, a baby is born is the next wagon, bringing the soul of the deceased person back in his or her next life. While you think the person is dead and gone, he or she is actually already starting another life.

In our life we evolve, and over many lives we evolve even more, so we move from one wagon to the next in that long train, pulling many, many wagons...many, many lives.

Our good and bad actions in previous lives create our present life conditions. So too our current good and bad actions will create the conditions

8. Your life, your existence and reincarnation.

of your next life. In this way we model our own future, that's why we are forever linked to our past actions.

The beauty of the idea is that nothing ever stops. You leave the scene, and you come back in another costume, another role to play, and all the people you love and live with are likely to be part of your soul group, so that you can evolve with them over time, simply in a new configuration each time, each life.

When you say goodbye to someone in life, remember, it's only temporary. In the afterlife and in a new life, there are plenty of possibilities to bring you back together.

If love is the prime quality we need to cultivate in our spiritual evolution, if such is the importance of love, then it is also logical and fair that what is made of love is indestructible and lasts throughout time.

Try to imagine it, try to imagine that things could be true without being able to see or touch them, or to have tangible proof. Turn off your brain and listen with your heart and see if you can find sense in this for yourself.

But of course, you don't have to, nobody can oblige you to believe anything other than what you want to believe and what you're comfortable with. You are free, for now and forever.

9. The hidden gift behind our sacrifices, struggles, and suffering.

Sometimes I wonder what our real job is. Is it that eight-hour-a-day job we get paid for, or the twenty-four-hour-a-day life job we do with our heart?

We can change our daytime job if we want to do something else, but we can't undo the permanent occupation that our own life implies. Your life job is simply managing your life, and that is a job that only you can do.

This job keeps you running all the time, day and night shifts, with no weekends off, no vacation, no retirement even. What kind of a job is that? Well, it's your life! And you are the director. You are evaluated on everything you do, as well as all you don't, especially on your dealings with other people; loved ones, friends, colleagues, strangers, and so on.

Which one of the two is the most important job? The one that we do with our mind, our day job, or the one that we give everything we have to, all our time and energy, our life job? Of course, the work of our life is our life itself.

The life-job has no time to lose, it starts when you're still in the womb and your growing brain starts to receive all kinds of stimuli from and through your mother; emotions, sounds, voices, laughter, and music. You interact by moving around, staying quiet, or kicking the walls.

Over the next years, you must realize that you were born, as a human being, on this planet floating somewhere in space and with a life expectancy of around eighty years.

9. The hidden gift behind our sacrifices, struggles, and suffering.

You find out basically that you got to a place where you're trapped in a body. You're alive but only for a finite amount of time before your show shuts down again. That's a pretty hard awakening when you first realize it. I remember thinking about these things when I was around twenty.

Next to starting earlier, the life-job runs late too, to the very end of your life, and you must also deal with all the existential questions. It's a tough job.

In life, you must learn how to walk, talk, read, write, and study. You go through high school, college, university, be a wife or a husband, a parent, and then, when you finally get the job you wanted, the hard work really starts. Up to then, you were just warming up.

Imagine for a minute, you got the job you wanted so much, you work hard, you study more, you're doing great, you're very dedicated, you're very successful. Only, you worked too hard, you neglected your work-life balance, you're only forty-five, and you got a heart attack, fall on the floor and die, just like that.

That's it, your life ends right there. It happens every day, we just don't imagine it happening to us.

Now, all the good that you were capable of in your life; your expressions of love, of care, of kindness, of friendliness, of compassion, and all the efforts and sacrifices you made, do you believe that it all vanishes just like that, that nothing of the incredible enterprise that we call life, perdures after death?

With the beauty of creation that we witness in nature in my mind, the idea of nothingness after death is inconceivable to me.

What do we say to people that struggled their whole life with disease; people that endured a life of hardship and of suffering and still went the distance?

Do we say to them, "In the end, you just die, you will have gained nothing, you will go back to nothing. All you did out of love even is meaningless."?

To people that made it through hardship and suffering, we say that their efforts are seen and recognized. A warm welcome will await them when their time comes, for they probably advanced greatly, paying the bills through their own sweat and tears.

Although their earthly life might have been miserable, from above, it will most likely be seen as very fruitful, because difficult lives pay off more karma, and their efforts counterbalance previous actions, clearing the way for a better next life.

This is the sense I make of it. If we don't believe that, then what's there to live for? There would be no reason to continue living when our life becomes too difficult. When you believe all the good you did will go up in smoke in the end anyway, what's the use? What's the purpose? Why continue?

Well, we do continue because that's what people do. Even when everything is difficult, and we are struggling, fortunately, we have the inner voice that tells us to continue, not to give up. We know at a deeper level that we must keep trying because we are part of something divine, something universal, and somehow our story continues.

When we don't give up doing our best, doing good, when we fight for something noble, then we are creating beauty, and in that role, we are at our best.

10. How to deal with a crisis?

Though we prefer to talk about other things, crises happen in our lives. Who has never been through one?

It is difficult to imagine that any adult person actually says that he or she has never had any moment of crisis. It seems unavoidable.

Today, we can expect to live, on average, around 80 years. Even if we make it to 90 years, it is reasonable to assume that we have been challenged by gradual physical decline.

This systematic decline is the smoothest way; you take little blows every now and then, but you can handle them, you keep standing. The pace at which the aging process unfolds is roughly at a rate most people can handle.

But a crisis happens when there's a sudden system overload, when we can't handle what's on our plate. This can happen to anyone, at any time; everyone is vulnerable. Even when you're asleep a personal disaster can hit you and change your life for good.

A terrible disease or, a serious accident, or any other unfortunate event can hit you really hard and set you back seriously. If you are lucky enough to come out of it, perhaps somewhat diminished, you might find that your new physical reality might not allow you to go back and live the life you had before. You suffer a physical and a mental blow simultaneously. Imagine how difficult such a disastrous event must be.

How do you cope with that? What can you do when something terrible overcomes you? It seems so difficult that we can ask ourselves, "Is there anything at all that we can do to overcome these types of dramatic events?"

The solution to a problem is always on a higher level. If the problem is on the physical level, then you must try to reason it out within your mind. If you are suffering mentally, then you should try to take in spiritual wisdom to deepen your insight and calm the mind.

With a better understanding of life, we see its functionality. Events such as losing a loved one of older age can be best seen as an inescapable reality of life because people come and go on this planet every second.

Other types of misfortune that "overcome" us might be best interpreted in the light of our spiritual evolution, to try to make sense of it. But I admit even if we try to do so, we often remain speechless in front of all the sad, terrible, and devastating news that comes to us in this increasingly chaotic world.

We're entering a noble enterprise when we step away from judging, and see through the physical scene that plays out in front of us, and attempt to construct meaning from what might initially seem bad luck or chaos. It is like bringing light into darkness. When we succeed in attributing meaning to a difficult situation, especially one that touches us deeply, it's an honorable effort and helps us on our path toward acceptance.

Coming back to the aging question, we can ask ourselves how to deal with it. When the aging process and its challenging consequences bring us down, we can say to ourselves, that although we got weaker physically over time, we got stronger mentally and hopefully wiser spiritually.

10. How to deal with a crisis?

But one's "spiritual life expectancy" is much more important than the physical one because it is the very reason for living and also the objective of our life.

Fulfilling one's spiritual life expectancy is serving your life-plan well, respecting the contracts with all parties involved, and so, being able to create beauty all along the way. All the beauty you were able to create you will take along as flowers in a splendid bouquet to present upon arrival.

The pay-off of succeeding to sail smoothly through the aging process is to be found in all the spiritual truths, riches, and treasures you constructed bit by bit over time that increased your level of consciousness.

We can also go one step further and add, that the time that passes ensures there's a beginning and an end to our life, because it's one more experience our soul takes on each time it incarnates, and one more experience it adds to one's overall spiritual journey when one excarnates.

When the business that you came to do in life is over and done with, then you've lived through your assignment, and you might as well return to base, to headquarters, to discuss your progress and review it with your mentor (or any other soul assigned to you).

Aging, however, is still a way of physical deterioration that we can anticipate, but when you have suffered a serious accident or when you have been diagnosed with a terrible disease or anything of that magnitude, then what do you do? What can you say?

However difficult it can be to keep calm in the most challenging situations, I still believe that as long as there is life and that somebody is conscious, the experience is important for your life experience, for things don't happen just like that, nothing happens without a reason.

You can go one step further and say that even when a person is in a coma, although the physical body is motionless, unconscious, you can only wonder about what the soul might be doing. I take it that the soul is on active duty, even when the physical body and the brain show a state of coma.

Even when nothing appears to be going on, a lot might be happening. It's like that perfectly tranquil lake, but you don't know what's going on beneath the surface.

Even when you are diminished, nailed to a hospital bed, you can score. I have seen my own father do that so many times in the last months of his life. I was impressed and admired him for it.

In spite of his pain and difficulty, he prepared tough questions to ask the medical staff about his own delicate situation, and at the same time, was thankful for every glass of water given and maintained high standards of courtesy. That's power.

I witnessed it, yes sadly from my earthly point of view, but saw it too, at the same time, from a spiritual perspective. I am sure that his efforts were seen and noted, of being kind and respectful, even when you are struggling for your life.

The tougher the situations you face, the harder the decisions are to make, and you often face them alone, in the lonely hours of your life. Yet those are also the moments that you can choose to transform misery into beauty.

10. How to deal with a crisis?

How? By choosing the noblest action, taking the highest path, perhaps the most difficult for you to do, but like this, you bring yourself one step closer to grace and bliss, to help from above.

When I find myself in a challenging situation, I ask myself: "What's the greatest risk in this situation?" Then I try to accept whatever I think that it is. I don't say I can accept it, but I try. I say to myself: "You're here now, but from here on, things might get more difficult. If they do, then what do you do?"

I also try to anticipate the most unfortunate outcome and ask myself if I could accept that. Why? First of all, a realistic inner dialogue helps. Secondly, it's a first step in the direction of acceptance, which doesn't mean that it makes it easy.

The best way to cope is to arm yourself with spiritual wisdom, so that you can explain the phenomena of life to yourself in the first place, and then serve others with it.

So, I prepare myself beforehand for possibly an unfortunate scenario, and then I step in the situation knowing what I might lose. When I do lose, I already made a first step toward accepting that loss.

This is not accepting defeat before the game even begins. It is reducing pressure or stress to a more manageable level, a level that doesn't incapacitate you. In this manner, it allows you to put things in perspective, to be realistic, and then when you re-enter the situation, you still give it your best shot, with reduced fear and/or anxiety, and so, a better inner chemistry to face the situation to be dealt with.

How do you deal with life's most challenging situations? How do you process an immediate life-threatening situation? Then what can you do? You accept the fact that you could die, because that might be real. But what can you do, when you are in such a delicate position?

First, you can and surely will break down, even, over and over again, but that's only normal. Let it be, accept it ... it will take time to get emotionally accustomed to the news, to get passed the initial shock.

Then, when the overwhelming emotion seems to subside somewhat, you can say to yourself: "I'm still here, and if my life has some purpose then I have no more time to waste on superficialities, because I don't know how much time I have left."

"I'm conscious, I can still think, my thoughts are my show now, my decisions are my act. This is what I still can control, this is my new job, and this is what I must concentrate on, this is where I am wanted to concentrate on. Because you are keenly observed when you are in difficulty, that's your prime-time moment here above."

Always when one is put in great distress, higher intelligence instantly knows, even before you do, and accompanies you, from behind the veil, whether you know it or not. Even in difficulty, try to maintain the highest and noblest thoughts. Engage only in the most beautiful actions, for they are in reality what you are, and are the symbolic fruits and flowers you bring with you when you finally go home, to the here above.

11. Unlearning the habit of comparing ourselves to others.

In life, there are many things that we must learn, and much of our learning is done through observational learning or role modeling. We look at others and try to do what they do; we often imitate practical behaviors that solve a specific problem.

Much later on in life, there might come a time when for some, it would be wiser to unlearn certain behaviors when they prove to have become counterproductive.

I think it is a fact of our social life that at least once in a while, we compare ourselves and our situation to that of other people. It is something that we do automatically as if we can't help it, it has become a habit.

Habits are learned behaviors, and it is normal that we were introduced to and confronted with the comparing mechanism at an early age when it was logical, functional, and necessary even.

We were compared and evaluated during the course of our development as a child, and then in school, or in a music class, or in a sports club. But as we grow older, and the differences between people's social positions grow as well, the endless comparing can become difficult to bear.

We tend to see the grass of our neighbor as always greener than our own, right? Well, perhaps we shouldn't even be looking at his grass, because it brings us only headaches. We might be better off minding our own business, because managing our own show is already difficult enough.

In general, knowing when to mind your own business can actually serve as a protection. It keeps you focused on your own story and keeps non-pertinent issues out of your sight. In this way, it doesn't unnecessarily stimulate or burden your mind, adding only to the restlessness we might all sometimes experience in our hectic lives.

When we do turn to comparing ourselves, we can be sure we're on the road to frustration and to feeling unhappy. Why? Because after your comparison is done, you're left to deal with the feeling that something is missing in your life. That realization might bring you down.

When we act not in alignment with spiritual principles, we shouldn't be surprised if our energy goes low. See it as a tiny inner revolution, as to make us realize we are on the wrong track.

We all have things that are not perfect in our lives, but it is better to count our blessings, and work with the reality of what we do have, instead of looking at what is real for somebody else, and part of a situation that isn't our own, and never will be.

If we would want to compare justly, then we would be less picky with whom and what item we choose to compare. We often don't compare the things that we have more of ourselves, we make sure we look at the things we don't have.

Often our comparisons are quick and superficial and deal with material things. If we would also take into account the less appealing elements of your neighbor's situation (the one with the green grass for example), then a more careful study would soon show us, that he too, found the same kind of surprises in his life bag as we did.

11. Unlearning the habit of comparing ourselves to others.

You can be sure, if your neighbor is a human being, then he has the same kind of problems, but we didn't see those, we were too busy staring at his green grass!

The fact of the matter is that comparing to others is an effective roadblock to our spiritual growth, because we are simply comparing the incomparable.

It makes no sense, especially seen from a higher level, because although we are similar in form, we cannot be alike. We each have a unique karmic heritage accumulated over time that shapes our future conditions, experiences, and life lessons.

Picture the entire human population walking on an endless road, yes billions of people, and still, every person walking separately, in his own spot and at his own pace. We all have the same starting point in this enterprise, and the same destination; reunification with the divine, but each and every one of us is at a different point in his or her evolution.

This fact changes everything, and makes each person perfectly unique, and so, incomparable.

Every person has a unique set of innate physical and mental abilities to start off with in life, a base from which you can build. These abilities are nurtured also again in a unique way by our environment, developing the abilities into qualities; transforming one's potential into concrete capabilities and learned behaviors. In this manner, huge differences between people are created.

Then, another crucial point is that no two people will have an identical or comparable life-plan, related to personal unfinished business from previous lives and to where each one of them stands in their path of evolution. Although the life-plan is subject to change because we have our free will, it's still reasonable to assume that at least some patterns in our life, if not some major events, are set to take place. If not, the whole idea of a life-plan would be false.

Any two people are not meant to be equipped alike, for their lives cannot be the same.

One has issues that must be still worked out with specific people, the other has other lessons to learn in other areas. Although the ingredients of our individual mix are quite the same, none are identical, we are all unique mixes.

When we take this into account and we realize our uniqueness, it functions as if we all have slightly different glasses on when looking at our world.

Despite our common physical features, we are all of distinct composition, and interpret our world subjectively, and so, our own experience can never be identical to that of another person.

For all these considerations, we are better off focusing on ourselves, on what we think is important for us to accomplish in our lives, and striving to do as well as we possibly can. All the best to you.

12. You are unique, you are the hero of your life.

In any regular life, we have things that we are happy with and things that we're not so happy with. But what can we do when things suddenly become more difficult, when problems and worries pile up?

Focus on what is on your plate and accept the problems as if you're not even surprised that they're there. Problems are inherent to life, and the specific problems you encounter reveal the areas where you still need to grow.

The degree of difficulty of your problem is proportional to your capacity to solve it, as the degree of hardship is proportional to what you can handle, to what you can carry, to what you can endure.

Nothing is put on our plate with the intention to lastingly hurt us or to break us. Ultimately, all earthly problems can be dealt with by adopting the right state of mind.

The right state of mind is always the spiritual state of mind, looking at it from above, standing above it, putting things back in the spiritual perspective, where everything belongs and all answers can be found.

Every person has a life-plan, like a scenario that foretells the story of your life to be, only you don't know this. Although much is flexible, left to your free will, I believe that at least some crucial events are set, and problems are often a part of the package. Everything depends on your karma. But, since it's your life-plan, no worries, because you are perfectly fit to deal with it.

I believe there is order in the universe and that you are given this life as an opportunity for growth, and you willingly accepted the total package with its tasks and challenges. You even agreed to deal with the problems that you are facing now. You also agreed to do your best, because why would you reincarnate if you knew in advance that you don't have what it takes to do the job?

Isn't it better to tell yourself you came here to be a winner? This life you have is a negotiated deal between you and the universe. At the end of your life, once reunited, you will review it and see what beauty you could make of your situation and your conditions. So, when you look at your current problems, ask yourself, as a hero would, what the noblest action would be for you to best deal with the situation at hand.

You are not only uniquely fit to play this role, you are also uniquely equipped with the exact qualities you need. You were tailor-made for this life, your life.

Over many, many lives, we are meant to accomplish our spiritual evolution; in just one life, it's the same principle, but on a smaller scale. Our evolution depends on the principles we adopt in life; the qualities we cultivated, the love we expressed, the compassion we showed, and the sharing with others that we were capable of.

To become the hero in your life, you must be decisive, choose righteous action, make efforts, and accept sacrifices. If you can engage your life with such a positive, spiritual attitude, you can turn negative situations into positive ones; turning something that seemed hopeless and lost into a beautiful learning experience that contributed significantly to your spiritual evolution.

12. You are unique, you are the hero of your life.

Along the way in your life, you will find each time you stand before misfortune, loss, or any type of challenge, that your mind can make the difference by making the right choice.

Panicking and letting oneself be overwhelmed by drama only extends the suffering. Repeating to oneself that you're in a disaster scenario only adds despair and reinforces the feeling of loss and failure. Instead, try to see in this hardship the opportunity for growth and decide to make the best of things.

Life is only experience, whatever happens in it, however disastrous events might get, you will still continue to exist! You are much more than only this one life.

Look carefully at the problem standing in front of you, then choose where you want to focus on, which reading of the problem you want to take along with you, which subjective version you want to hear echoing in your mind as you move on.

It's a matter of how you choose to process the problem, the issue, the experience, because your subjective interpretation will emotionally charge the association or the memory that you will store and carry along with you.

If you are strong and do your best to make sense out of seeming disorder, you might come to see that throughout your life when you were put to the test, and did your best, higher forces were right beside you all the time.

If you can see even further, you might feel that you are wanted and encouraged to surpass yourself by responding to painful experiences with righteous actions.

We all have spiritual guides that try to help us. Perhaps you received help with accepting the idea that your problems are there for a reason, thus helping you to put things into perspective. Helping you get yourself together, find the courage to go back to work and do your best in a new chapter of your life.

The help we receive can be in the smallest realizations, the little steps you make in the right direction helping you understand things better. This is the most precious help we can get.

All these little steps combined, will make a leap forward in the end. Help from above doesn't always come in the form we prefer. Things cannot simply be solved for you. To become the hero of your life, you will have to play that part yourself.

We also must see that we create our own problems, we create now the exact nature of our future life lessons. In the same way, the life lessons we face today are of the kind that we previously showed to be in need of. We are ourselves responsible for our current conditions.

With time, we come to see that the help we received all along the way came to us perhaps through increased understanding of life, precious spiritual realizations, and a stronger intuition. All of these contribute to a greater appreciation of the gift of life we received from above to help us on our path of spiritual evolution.

The goal of life is the acts of love you showed and the precious pearls of wisdom you carry along with you into eternity.

In terms of our spiritual evolution, you may not decide where you will go, but you may decide how you want to get there. You can choose a challenging shortcut or an annoying roundabout way, or something in

12. You are unique, you are the hero of your life.

between, but the goal of reunification with the divine stands at the end of the program for all. Therefore, you cannot undo the fact that you must learn, but you may decide the pace of your progress.

In our life, the same principle seems to apply. We might feel we have no control over all that happens to us, but we are free to decide how to react.

If you want to be a spiritually smart human being keen on advancing, then you might start by realizing that right from when you were young, in many Western cultures, society has put us on the wrong foot. We shouldn't look at our life in terms of all that we want to get out of it, but exactly the opposite, about what our input is.

We may speak of human beauty in life when one is able to commit one's personal resources to upgrade one's own conditions and at the same time contribute significantly to the common good.

Whether you realize it or not, every minute you're alive you're on stage, performing. You might think, "My life is ordinary and of interest to no one", but you should know you're right in the spotlight, playing your part, in the middle of your show.

Play your life as well as you can, play it like a hero.

13. Building one's spiritual understanding.

The universe wants us to grow, so what does it do? It puts challenges on our path of evolution, not to break us, but to burden us to the extent we can handle, what we are capable of carrying.

Why? Because we are not simply here to be happy, but rather to learn. Unless challenged, we remain less inclined to learn, less willing to change our ways.

Spiritual understanding permits us to see beyond the usual haphazard explanations of life events.

I believe in the intended beauty of a human life, the sacredness of life, and in the functionality of all the time we have in our life. If we meet an obstacle on our way, it is because we apparently needed to experience whatever the obstacle will bring. Perhaps we were on the wrong track?

When we are stopped in our tracks, we are meant to think and ask ourselves if something was wrong or if there is a reason for this happening here and now.

Next to, karmic considerations, the obstacle was probably believed to be a more effective learning mechanism, than a more carefree path.

A successful life is not measured simply by how happy you actually were. Instead, it is determined by all we could learn, all we could change about ourselves that needed to be changed, and all the love we were able to demonstrate.

13. Building one's spiritual understanding.

In the end, after your life-show is over and you're back in the heavens, you will very likely understand the reason or even the necessity behind all the difficult moments in your life, and you will be perfectly in peace with it. Such is the perfection of the universe.

We, as souls in human form, are fabulous beings designed for spiritual growth, self-realization, enlightenment, and reunification with the divine. Yet, we are using the time in our life less and less for these intended purposes.

The spiritual dimension in general, whether that be practice or theory, is no longer what it once was. We can look back even at ancient cultures and see how greater importance was given to the spirit world and the afterlife.

In our modern times, we generally use our minds for simpler things. This shows you that time pushes certain things into the background for some period while new things emerge. Everything is constantly changing, and with time, our view on things changes.

But we can't deny our spiritual identity as souls by simply neglecting it, or by simply looking the other way. We actually might feel sorry at the moment of passing, and beyond, when we realize that, in our life, we didn't give it much attention, if such was our decision.

We also see in our lives that time helps us evolve naturally. Things that you thought important at the age of twenty no longer take that same place in your mind when you're thirty, and by the age of forty, they will have moved even further into the background.

In this manner time can be seen as an ally that helps you grow in your thinking while growing older. Typically, when you're forty, and living consciously, you don't want to go back to thinking what you thought when you were twenty, because you have evolved since then.

Finetuning one's ideas and opinions, or even revising completely one's point of view, was such a considerable effort, it's only normal you value the fruits of your labor.

In this way, by understanding its functionality, you overcome that time issue. You turn a menace into an asset and a challenge into victory. You are given life to experience the things you need to experience, and you are meant to educate, cultivate and coach yourself in a manner that enables you to give each time a 'higher' or more humane response to the experiences and challenges you find on our path.

Challenges, obstacles, and problems can sometimes trigger the greatest decisions in your life. When things are really difficult for example, you might decide to move to a different country, with a different job and a new life, and perhaps, this turns out to be a magic move, changing your life for the better.

The most difficult moments of your life are sometimes looked back upon as crucial turning points that needed to take place to change a situation that came to maturity, that could no longer be. Something that was always unimaginable suddenly becomes possible when you are forced to make a move.

In unusual, or even extreme situations, we are forced to take bold action, something we are less likely to do when we are absorbed in our daily routine, living our sweet life.

A difficulty might make you suffer but overriding is what you can and will do with it. It is much about what it triggers inside of you. Does it

13. Building one's spiritual understanding.

make you slip into depression and shut yourself off from the outside world, or does it push you to dive deep into your feelings and perhaps find great inspiration for a beautiful painting?

Sometimes, a problem presents itself to help you. For example, when you have left an issue unattended for a long time, and then suddenly, you are forced to make a decision.

By making the right changes, one can sometimes change the meaning of one's entire life while also making a positive contribution to other people's lives. The hidden gift in misfortune is that it is meant to start a process that will bring you increased awareness, and higher consciousness. There is nothing greater to be obtained or harvested in life.

The same principle applies to physical challenges. You can be so physically challenged that you practically can't do anything anymore. However terrible this must be, you can still be the hero of your life by choosing to be righteous in your thoughts and actions and having the strength to put it into practice.

What does the hero do then? He chooses righteous action. Though he may be losing his body, he is not being "conquered" by anything or anybody, he is still mentally fit, untouched, independent, and invincible. Our life is not about being physically fit, it's about developing our consciousness.

All you need to be a hero is a conscious mind. As long as you can still think, you are still playing the game. Every second counts and has its importance in your life.

14. Collective consciousness: The state of the world.

In the beginning, we were only a few people on this planet. Over time, with more and more people around, we started to scatter across the globe, to each have our own land and to establish our own camps, building our own villages, and forming our own nations.

We quickly understood that to survive or even just keep what you had, you needed to protect yourself from the outside world, not so much from the wild animals, but more from your fellow man. So, we started to build walls around our villages and fortresses and castles for protection.

With time, we saw war. Naturally, wars occurred when we were attacked and when we needed to defend our community, our belongings, and all we built through hard work. Unfortunately, wars were also started against weaker peoples, when victory on the battlefield was assured before even drawing the sword.

It was simply an opportunity to be seized, to conquer more land, to take what could be taken, to gain more influence, and to have more power. For a long time, the world proved to be a grewsome place, where unimaginable atrocities were committed between peoples, between nations, between man and his fellow man.

When we look at our world today, we still see the same problems between nations, between peoples. The old battlefields still exist, but acts of war also commonly take place in our streets, schools, shopping malls, neglected neighborhoods, where people kill each other for small profits and battle over territory to expand their trade.

14. Collective consciousness: The state of the world.

Nations still compete for dominance, to influence other nations, to further the interests of the group of people they represent. Countries still use nuclear weapons, as a deterrent, but also to pressure and manipulate. Sometimes even biological and chemical weapons are developed on the side.

At the height of the Cold War, Russia and the United States had enough nuclear power to destroy mankind 13 times over. Looking at all of this, we can conclude that there still is a lot of ignorance. Some "world leaders" as we call them, seem to have no clue as to why they are on this planet, and what efforts they are supposed to make to try to get along with one's neighbor.

But even though things look difficult, the mission that we have as mankind, to increase our level of consciousness, remains unchanged. It only becomes more difficult to turn things around, to put the world machine in reverse.

If life is given to us to evolve spiritually, to show our capacity to love, do we realize how far we have gone in the opposite direction? If this is indeed our collective track-record as a world population, what evaluation could we expect? I let you decide for yourself.

I believe that the peaceful co-existence of all peoples of the world is a collective task for all of us, but if nations around the world don't wake up and review their ideas and policies, it will be difficult to get there.

We can't just sit still and wait until our leaders come to sense. People make up nations and we must come to recognize our own individual responsibility in the way we see and treat our neighbor and in what manner we can individually contribute to making life on this planet a little bit gentler.

I once heard Peter Gabriel, a famous British artist, say: "Man's evolution can be measured by what he includes in the concept of 'we.'" This phrase brings us right to the heart of the problem. Think about it, if you will.

15. Our successes and failures seen in the light of our spiritual evolution.

Experiences of failure and experiences of success, do they not amount to quite the same in the end? Is it just the time passing by that straightens out the differences between them? It might sound crazy when you have just won a boxing match to hear someone say "in the end, winning is the same as losing."

But imagine your life being filmed, the cameraman zooming out until looking at you from far above, from high in the sky, from the afterlife point of view. Then, the play-back mode shows you the highs and the lows of your past life and all the different states of mind you were in with respect to these experiences.

You see that the beauty you could create, often came to you in the lonely hours and moments of your life, when you were receptive and inspired, and thankful for all you could enjoy in your life. All was pure. You see also perhaps that when success came, it brought you perhaps new friends, but the topics of discussions somehow often dealt with material or superficial things, and less with the essentials of life like before.

You now see how these events influenced you, and you see the mechanism at work over time, you see your own growth process unfolding in slow motion. Then while looking at your life from this point of view, repeat to yourself once more, "in the end, winning is the same as losing," and chances are you will be less startled by it, seeing both what success and victory brought you and what failure and defeat did.

In the end, both are reduced to experience, yes, at first sight of opposite nature, but when we zoom out even further to consider our total existence, they come together. In retrospect they boil down to experiences that made us who we are today, each one influencing us at a specific moment in time and in a specific way, to create an ever-enriching experience.

The value of your life is not to be found in one specific event or experience; it is to be found in the entire life process. You can be a heavy weight boxing champ at 30 years, but if your life doesn't end there, the process continues.

As the champ grows older and becomes a granddad, and reaches old age, he will have had so many other significant experiences that will have impacted him, that the "weight" of his title is considerably reduced by the time the champ hits his final hour.

Next to that, we must hope that his boxing career at least helped him to become a gentler person on the inside!

We generally don't only have wins or losses on our track record, but a mix of them. Winning all the time can make you lazy and having never won can bring out the pitbull in you.

All to say that it is arguable that in a certain way, winning could prepare you for losing and losing could prepare you for winning.

If there is truth in this, then winning and losing are merely different points on the same wheel, and they come together to contribute in the formation process of you as a person all throughout your life.

If you would have to make and present a cake at the end of your life, representative of your entire life, then your victories, defeats, successes, and failures would all be there, as the different ingredients of that cake.

15. Our successes and failures seen in the light of our spiritual evolution.

Victory and defeat would become indistinguishable from one another as they melt together, both as ingredients, during the making and baking of the cake. Their importance as separate experiences fades away into the background.

They transform and unite to be part of the creation of something greater, something bigger that cares no more about the exact ingredients, but focuses on the beauty of the cake.

Showing us that seemingly unrelated experiences shouldn't be regarded as merely stand-alone events, accomplishments or failures, because they set the stage in a particular way for the next event, shaping a person's character accordingly.

The supposed separateness of experiences washes away like footprints in the sand, when one considers that all experiences build on one another and maintain a dynamic inner climate of continuous change and adaptation, as all new life events are integrated to the aggregate of life experiences.

We must neither show off our successes and inflate our ego nor over-dramatize our losses and suffer from feelings of inferiority.

All experience is temporary, always passing to fade into the background, making place for new ones to take center stage.

Each life experience will add another link to a long chain of total life experiences of your soul's evolutionary journey over time. All serving the higher purpose of spiritual evolution.

16. How not to judge and label at once every event in our life?

Many of us have accustomed ourselves to going through life judging and labeling everything that happens to us as it happens. "This is good, that is bad, that's great, and that's terrible". We must see that although we put a specific label on events right as they happen, time might shed a different light on the event and possibly change its meaning.

We could see if we could cultivate ourselves to be more even-minded as to the things that happen to us. If we could refrain from labeling events at once, it could turn out to be a wise quality.

When we do not judge everything at once, we pre-acknowledge implicitly the yet to be discovered flaws in all that appears to us as good at first sight, as well as the hidden flowers that time might make us see in all that seems undesirable.

Even-mindedness would be a welcome attribute to cultivate in our hectic world. As we are often too close up on things, too emotionally involved, learning to look at the events of our lives more as observers, might enable us to function better.

I would like to tell you this parable of the Chinese farmer and show you how he reacts to the events in his life.

Once there was a Chinese farmer, and although he lived simply, he owned a horse that helped him work his land and pull heavy loads. One day his horse escaped through an opening in the fence and ran away.

16. How not to judge and label every event in our life?

The villagers that came by said, "Oh your horse is gone, what a terrible situation for you!"

The farmer, while staring at them, remained emotionless and said, "Perhaps."

The next morning, when he woke up, he found his horse grazing in front of the farm, with two other horses that he had apparently brought along.

The villagers that passed by later that day, saw three horses grazing, and said: "Incredible! Your horse came back with two more horses. How lucky you are!"

The farmer remained unemotional, saying, "Perhaps."

The next day, his twenty-year-old son tried to mount one of the new horses and fell off the horse and broke his leg.

The villagers that had heard the news came by and said, "Gee, your son broke his leg, now you have no more help, how terrible!"

He stood there with the same even-mindedness and again simply said, "Perhaps."

The next day, the Chinese army made a surprise visit to the village, because they needed young soldiers. Many were taken, but not the farmer's son because of his broken leg.

Some of the villagers that had their sons taken away passed by that day and said, "How lucky you are to still have your son at home!"

And so on, and so on…

Many of us know that we label things right as they happen, while it might be still unclear what effect an event will have on us, still we automatically put a value judgment on it. It seems irresistible.

Of course, I'm not talking about tragic events that we logically label as terrible, but rather the smaller events of which the impact can be reversed by an event of opposite nature, as clearly shown in this little parable.

By reframing, or putting in a different light, what might at first seem an unharmonious event in your life, you might succeed in keeping your calm and accepting it for what it really is; a learning opportunity, a steppingstone, to structure and strengthen ourselves spiritually. Then, with calmness, but with no less resolve and courage, you can still do your best to solve the problem, or to improve your situation.

The Chinese farmer didn't even reframe the events in his life, he went one step further and just suspended his judgement. He left things open by saying "Perhaps," He had no problem with it, there was no rush, he accepted the events, each time, as just another fact of life.

When we stop to judge things all the time and don't label things right away, we create a less hectic internal environment, that is, we discipline ourselves by not at once equating uncertainty with insecurity.

Perhaps the Chinese farmer was looking at the bigger picture, seeing the string of events over time, the process of things, and not focusing on any particular event in itself. If we look at the process with a spiritual eye, we can see perhaps the unfolding of a divine plan.

16. How not to judge and label every event in our life?

Perhaps the horses and his son breaking his leg served the higher cause of keeping his son out of the Chinese army? Events that could seem at first sight unrelated might take on new meaning when seen from a distance. They might even become significant, as they naturally fall in place in your mind, according to your own intuition and interpretation.

17. How to raise society's level of consciousness?

We must face the fact that our society is fascinated by violence and crime. Many of the most successful movies and television series we make are stories about violence and crime. These are not movies that simply have scenes of violence and crime in them, no, the viewer is taken by the hand, to experience the movie through the eyes of the main character, which is often the gangster.

We are naturally led to identify ourselves with him, and consequently, in our mind, the gangster becomes our hero, and if we find him really cool, he might even become an alternative role model.

When we choose to make a movie about crime, with great and beautiful actors, and sell it to most countries around the world, we are contributing to the blurring of shared concepts of what's right and what's wrong, of what's righteous action and what's wrongful action.

Especially for children and teenagers, it can be confusing when we see our best actors, respected and loved by so many, kill people left and right on the screen.

It might be wiser for us as a society, to cut down our consumption of violent and crime-related entertainment. Why? Because we have to look further ahead as a society and ask ourselves what we want to become, and in that light, look and see where we are currently headed.

Shouldn't we try to inspire people differently, especially teenagers and young adults? Why can't we make more movies about people that contribute positively to society?

17. How to raise society's level of consciousness?

In case we do want to evolve as a society, we must understand that we should rather promote higher human values, than portray actions on the screen that nobody should be doing and that neither actors nor producers would want to be a victim of in their own real life.

We must realize that what we look at on our screen, somehow corresponds with us. You are not only what you eat, you are what you watch too. The scenes we watch linger on in our mind after the show, and then in our dreams. What we choose to watch is where we put our precious time and attention, and in this way, it becomes part of us, of what we are.

How? Well, when you're watching a one-and-a-half-hour movie, how many scenes of violence and crime does your mind take in and store? Your unconscious mind is like a sponge, it will absorb what you pay attention to. While it may seem that you forget most of what you're seeing, your unconscious mind does not. It stores images and scenes, or fragments of them, in your "system."

When the movie is over and you want to go to sleep, your unconscious mind just terminated downloading the movie. Now, when you actually fall asleep your mind starts to process and store new information, including the scenes of that movie.

In your dreams or nightmares (depending on the quality of the movie), some deranging scenes might well come back to you, mixed with other stored material. This explains why dreams are often so weird and so difficult to understand.

One step further would be to say that the emotions provoked by these scenes (such as intense sudden fear) might at one time somehow affect you through an unconscious behavior modification. One day, you might unexpectedly become afraid of something, and you can't explain why.

Taking this into account, it follows that we shouldn't any longer continue to make movies about violence and crime on the same scale because it will pull us down. They will not lift us up.

It doesn't mean that we should make fewer movies, but we should shift the focus and make more movies about love, friendship, the beauty of nature, and so on, basically stories that display higher human values, because that would inspire people the right way, the way people need to be inspired in today's world.

A movie can include violence or crime when their omission would denaturalize the story because today, it seems the other way around. We feel we must put enough violence, crime, and explosions and then basically invent a story around it.

This being said, I believe that the job we have as mankind, to evolve spiritually, is our common mission. I think there are many spiritual people around the world that feel that the state of things in our world of today is kind of coming to maturity, meaning that things can't really go on much longer like this. Change is expected.

We don't know what, when, and how, but still, I think there's a growing feeling, almost a consensus I would say, that something important will happen. Something important is bound to happen sooner or later to start changing things for the better.

Think about this, if you will, and see if you can find a way to contribute to this process. Ask yourself if you feel there's a place for you to share your qualities in the most important common enterprise of this planet. That is, increasing the level of consciousness of humanity, saving humanity from itself.

18. Connecting to the internet and connecting to the Divine.

How to deal with the challenges of modern society?

Although we are generally happy to profit from new technological advances that facilitate our lives in a practical sense, there is sometimes also a downside to take into account.

Look how much time we spend on the internet; for professional reasons, for personal motivations, for convenience or out of necessity. So far, so good. Yet some people have lost their mastery over their time as they fell into the modern tech trap and became addicted to cellphone use, social media, and other internet applications, simply seeming unable to keep their screen time within reasonable limits.

In today's world, we see so many people living and breathing with their smartphones in their hand, continuously checking their internet connection and incoming text and voice messages.

These people tend to be less aware of their surroundings, and only 'half' present in the contact with their company.

Others may take numerous selfies a day and share them instantly with hundreds of social media "friends" or thousands of followers, but have no time left to communicate properly with their closest friends and loved ones.

You see friends or even family members sitting together at a table in a restaurant, everybody eyeing their cellphones. It's crazy. In this way, people that were close become strangers again.

Today people still sit next to each other, yet everybody is in his or her own bubble. You even think twice about making contact with any person holding a phone in front of his or her face because chances are that he or she doesn't want to be drawn away from the little screen.

Next time you find yourself in this type of situation, look how much time passes that people just don't move, not even in uncomfortable positions, just eyeing the screen and typing.

People are also constantly bombarded all day by messages, notifications, news alerts, and so on, giving them even less time left to think on their own, independently of their cellphone.

You must remain in the driver's seat of your life, deciding yourself how you spend your time. Cellphones and internet are great, they're only also very intrusive. We need lucidity and discipline to manage them, that's all.

If left unchecked, some people have no time left to invest in any one person anymore, because they are interested in everybody and everything at the same time. In the old days, we learned not to interrupt conversations between people, to respect other people's privacy, and to respect a person's peace of mind when taking a break, or even respecting one's own need to have a moment of tranquility.

But not our cellphone, it keeps on coming at you, beeping, buzzing, and jumping all over the table. Imagine what this does to your mind, it undermines your concentration, it disperses your attention, it interferes

18. Connecting to the internet and connecting to the Divine.

with your peace of mind, and rather causes restlessness, while we would be better off being like a calm lake on the inside.

Life is complicated enough, and we need to be able to think straight to make the best decisions. If you have something important to think over, to be able to concentrate on any subject, you must first already cut through the layers of distraction that are so plentiful in our external environment; people, cars, buses, trains, motorcycles, etc. Then there's your own internal stress; all the issues and problems that preoccupy us.

So, next to shutting yourself off from the outside world, you have to "park" all your personal issues somewhere mentally out of sight as well. Only then can you try to do some serious thinking.

If for your spiritual practice, you want to go even deeper, to see what your inner self can come up with when put in the right conditions, to possibly have an interesting train of thought or a precious realization, you need even more tranquility, and preferably a peaceful natural setting.

The most precious experiences will still come from yourself, from within, from your soul, from your connection with the Divine, and not from your cell phone with its internet connection.

We should try to balance things, balance our time between staying connected to the internet and being connected to ourselves, to our soul, to the divine.

19. How do many of us see our fellow man?

Today, some people look at their fellow man, study him, and wonder how to profit from him. When we have something to sell, we are glad if we succeed in talking people into buying our product, and rarely wonder after selling, if they're actually happy with it, if it brought them what we said it would.

Most products in tv commercials are presented by beautiful models that are not representative of the general public, and we are carefully manipulated to associate the product with beauty, with being successful, with having a nice car or with a beautiful house, basically, all things that most people aren't and/or don't have.

It is not the fact that we buy things that is upsetting; it's the way in which things are presented to us. The level of manipulation is so great, that we could ask ourselves if we believe that it's an honest way of relating to one another. The way in which we interact with one another reveals the way we see our fellow man, and it shows the quality of our mind and of our inner being.

Just as we can choose to see another person as an opportunity to better our conditions, we can also see that person as a colleague of life, as an opportunity to exchange about our life experiences, and enrich each another in this mutually beneficial process.

I encourage people to think about how they see their fellow man, and how they choose to communicate with other people, and specifically to mind all that we say to people. Everything you do, think and say builds

19. How do many of us see our fellow man?

continuously what you currently are, and what you are in the making, what you are becoming.

There are spiritual laws that govern us and every action has its consequence. If you persist in rightful action, for example, and discipline yourself in doing good, then sooner or later you will find yourself walking in the sunshine.

The working of these mechanisms is invisible, but still they are there, like when we check the time on our watch and neglect to appreciate the intricate clockwork hidden inside it that makes it happen.

Every day we look at what we find on our plate without wondering where it came from, but if you would analyze what you find on your plate, and if you would ask yourself if it could have a connection with earlier decisions or events in your life, you may discover the mechanisms in place underneath the surface of your visible world.

Understanding these mechanisms enables you to construct deeper meaning; deeper meaning that will sooner or later make you see that your life is a functional 'exercise' with indeed a plan and a purpose.

The reason for major events in our life could well have their origin in your life-plan, made up before you came back to this world. You can't recall this consciously, but under hypnosis, chances are that you could.

It is wise to be considerate, respectful and kind in our dealings with other people, because the quality of our person is shown in the way we deal with our environment, next to the obvious fact that we reap what we sow.

One could argue that the 'you reap what you sow' mechanism can't be observed, or proved, so why should we bother ourselves with it?

You might bother because even if you can't see the mechanics at work before your own eyes, you would still largely prefer to be pleasantly surprised by the return on your actions than seeing yourself slip into unpleasant situations here and there. We all very well know, when we do good and when we don't.

20. We are all busy, but are we busy doing the right things?

Unless we do the right things, the right things won't happen to us.

If you would ask an adult person, "What keeps you busy?" then this person might very well say,

"A demanding job, a family with two kids, keeping the house organized, doing the groceries, going shopping and eating out on Saturdays, and Sundays we often meet up with family or friends, or go places with the kids. Time just flies."

I reckon most people would say that this is a common weekly routine.

We understand that all of this keeps us busy, we can even argue that all this must be done to keep everything running. So true, but however logical, it still is a choice, because you still could choose to spend your time differently.

Why would we spend our time differently? Well, stand still and ask yourself what all this type of "busy-ness" accomplishes in the end, besides keeping things running?

Even though these activities contribute to the quality of your family life, and you are happy about that, the real question that remains is:

"How does your current lifestyle, that is, these choices of how you spend your time, serve you in the bigger picture? How do they contribute to the ultimate purpose of your life?"

If the purpose of our life is to grow spiritually, then we must engage in activities that better us as persons, that further our spiritual knowledge, that increase our awareness, that sharpen our meditation practice, all to enhance our individual and collective spirituality. We know that we can only spend our time once, and we must also see that the choices we make with our time have consequences.

The way we spend our time predisposes us, and conditions us. If you want to become a major tennis or soccer player and practice all the time, then, even in the moments you don't practice, you see the ball bouncing around in your mind, and you see yourself making the moves you're trying to master when practicing.

Your mind takes you further than your conscious actions. When you stop "balling around," your mind continues. Similarly, when you engage more often in meditation, with time, you are likely to become a calmer person.

It is a co-construction between yourself and the universe, much like a dance, and here on earth you were put to lead that dance. The more elegant your steps are, the finer the responses will be from the world around you, and the happier your life will be. A happy or harmonious life will allow for pleasant memories to be taken along into the afterlife, ensuring peace of mind.

Your actions and interactions have a ripple effect, they continue to exist, arguably forever. When you bump into a person that you haven't seen in a long time, your mind instantly retrieves the memories of your last

20. We are all busy, but are we busy doing the right things?

interaction with that particular person, and presents it with a distinct feeling attached to it, almost like a price tag.

It is logical that our past actions continue in our minds and bring back specific memories and a particular energy associated with it, re-actualizing the situation, putting the old into the new.

You can see this easily when at a reception or other social gathering, and you watch the host greet different people, and you see all the changes in facial expression, speech, general posture, specific body language and energy as the person receives one guest after another.

Your mind actualizes or updates information all the time, it is a mechanism that is continuously at work in our life. When we look at the many lives that we live, the same principle applies. Each time we come back, we come with the old experiences from all our past lives and draw upon acquired qualities from previous lives, from lessons already learned. That's why people with extraordinary qualities are sometimes referred to as 'old souls'. We re-actualize acquired qualities in a new setting, in a new life.

All to say, that, if the purpose of our life is to grow spiritually, to acquire ever more fine qualities as a person, and to work on raising your level of consciousness, then we could righteously ask ourselves-thinking back of that weekly routine mentioned before-, if we got our priorities set straight.

Because, unless we allocate some time to spiritual practice, contemplation, thought, prayer, study or anything of the kind, we are not likely to advance much on our spiritual path.

It's important to question oneself about one's choices in life, especially when one's well into adulthood.

When one does reserve some time for regular spiritual practice, the mechanism will start to work for you, and you will see that you will develop your abilities with increasing ease in the area of your choice.

Some come to realize, at an older age, that they needn't had to work so hard to build 'things' that can't be taken along with you into the afterlife, while they could have dedicated more time and effort to the high purpose of their life.

When you do put time aside to work on what is essential in your life, and on what you can take along with you into the afterlife, that is, your spiritual progress, then you are likely to harvest the fruits of your efforts.

The price to pay for not getting the priorities right might be felt as disappointment or frustration, as one might feel sorry when realizing you missed a precious opportunity. Our free will allows us to make our own choices, and our choices show what our priorities are in life.

It sounds nice to be free to make our own choices, but we are responsible for what we choose, because our choices do come back to us.

When we do not know what the purpose of our life is, it is not strange that we can end up spending our time focusing on what isn't essential while we think we're doing fine.

A hard awakening awaits us then, when we finally discover, after an entire life of hard work, that we bet on the wrong horse. We had thought we knew better and chose not to investigate and further our

20. We are all busy, but are we busy doing the right things?

spiritual knowledge. The reality that our true nature is soul, stands for all, no matter if you acknowledge this or not.

When you choose to dedicate much time and effort to your work, like many of us do, and you succeeded in doing well, even if you have attained material security or even complete financial independence, you're still not immune to the anxiety that the big questions of our life often provoke. Why am I here? What's next?, and so on.

Even when you're rich in a material 'comfort', the realization that the years of your life are ticking away, is surely less comfortable. Rich or poor can both be plagued by losing a parent, or having a child that is seriously ill, or anything else that can trouble you down here and that money can't simply buy you a way out of.

Being alive on this planet often means having to face some human drama, at least one's own drama. No one can escape that. It is wise, both from a spiritual point of view and a practical, to be fully aware of this reality because it can make you see that the power of money is only relative.

When one understands that the pursuit of solely material things is abusive to one's own very nature, it helps you to adjust the priorities in your life.

Some people can't be happy, because they suffer from themselves, from their own state of mind, from excessive mental turbulence. Some people have a hard time thinking positively, and when they indeed fail to do so, they suffer. We should do our best to stay in the right state of mind, as not to become in need of a wake-up call.

Unfortunate events like earthquakes, floods, wildfires, typhoons or tsunamis, can take your belongings away over night, but each hour you put in contemplating your life, going over the big questions of your existence, doing meditation and finetuning your connection to the above, you advance on your spiritual path, you invest in eternity, into your soul, where it's completely safe, where nothing and nobody can touch it.

That's why we hear the saying: "build your home on solid rock", on something eternal, on something real. When you invest in your soul, and in love and in wisdom, you are sure never to lose what you have built, not even when you pass into the afterlife.

Actually, at the moment of passing, and afterwards, you will be very pleased with all you did to further your knowledge and understanding of life, of why you are here and of what is expected of you. Special importance is given to what good you could do with all that was given or entrusted to you; your intellect, your qualities, your abilities, your time, your money, your energy, and so on.

On the contrary, when your time comes to pass over, you might be asked if you have anything to show of your life. If you have not at all lived consciously from a spiritual point of view, then you can only trust that you were a good person.

No worries, most people are good people, and good people will be well received. You will feel fine, but you might realize that you could have done more than being a good person, and that could have made your life outstanding.

Going out of your way for others and acting on what your heart indicates you to do, instead of blindly trusting man's rules and laws, is what could have earned you credit. Also, it is what you could learn about life and beyond that is valued and that matters, instead of all you could do for yourself and your own camp.

20. We are all busy, but are we busy doing the right things?

Putting off the most important issues of your life to be looked at when the end nears, will not earn you any prizes in the heavens. It most probably will earn you a return ticket to come back to live a similar life hoping that you will make different choices here and there, waiting for you to become more spiritually inspired.

In this light, my advice to any of us is to think twice to turn your head away when "life" offers you a chance to contemplate and exchange on spiritual issues, because I believe, it is nothing less than fundamental to succeed in one's life.

See every chance to enrich yourself spiritually, as if that opportunity were handed to you, created even by your own soul; begging you in this way to dedicate some time and thought to "spiritual questions".

If you decided you had better things to do in your life than to attend to spiritual matters, count on the possibility that you will be shown once you're above, your own decisions that kept you from advancing spiritually. As if you were filmed, you will watch yourself in play-back mode and relive the most significant moments when you made important decisions with your own free will.

A big surprise awaits people that didn't believe in anything while living their lives because when they die, they will realize instantly that they still exist, only without a physical body.

You are free to decide what you want, with your free will, and where you put your time and effort, and accordingly, there will be no doubt as to whom is responsible.

Wishing every one of you much wisdom in your decision-making.

21. Be your own spiritual coach:
In calmness, turn inward, and trust yourself.

Why would anyone need to try to be one's own spiritual coach?

First of all, because one's spiritual development is a very personal matter, one must find one's inner path, and one will have to learn to accompany oneself in this process anyway, even with a spiritual coach.

When we start in this life, we first have to listen to our parents, then we have to listen to our schoolteachers, then some listen even more to college or university professors, and then, when we get our first job, we often have to listen even more.

Basically, we were taught all along that learning and the construction of our knowledge, comes from the outside and not from within. We were conditioned this way, and it might seem natural by now, but it isn't.

It's only logical that we can be somewhat uncomfortable when trying to listen to ourselves because we haven't learned to listen to ourselves on a deeper level. Still, every human being has the innate ability to turn one's attention inward, and with time and practice, attune to the Divine, to the universe.

I don't know, but I imagine in earlier times, when our lives were less hectic and more in balance with nature, we were perhaps naturally more inclined to connect to the above. But nowadays we seem to give more importance to all the high-tech stuff that seems to have taken over our lives.

21. Be your own spiritual coach: In calmness, turn inward, and trust yourself.

If we could balance things a bit more, we could benefit greatly from retrieving this precious and essential ability that was once, perhaps quite naturally part of our skillset.

While most of what you have learned in the western traditional system will prove insufficient to help you further on your spiritual journey, here's a simple technique that you can try to become more receptive to that what might be within:

Simply sit still in a peaceful setting and then try to listen to yourself, to your inner voice. By calming the mind and introducing moments of meditation, one becomes more receptive to any form of inspiration and thereby develops one's intuition.

This technique, when practiced, will naturally become part of your way of life, and might help to make you calmer, helping you to accept things as they are, and with time and practice, it might help you to find the answers to the issues you are dealing with.

We see that in the light of coaching oneself spiritually, the best move you can make is to try to connect yourself in meditation to the all-knowing, the Divine, the universe.

Now you see, we're talking about something of a wholly different nature and importance than the subjects we normally study in school, in university, or even in most professional settings, because we are talking about our evolution as a soul, and this is an existential question and should be the highest priority in your life.

After you realize that you're a human being while you are on this planet and a soul while you are off this planet, you can ask yourself who you foremost want to be associated with; the human often ego-oriented person or the eternal soul?

On a deeper, unconscious level, you know very well who you are, but the 'high command' wants you to make the right choices in every life. Even if you are already beautifully engaged on your spiritual path, once you come down, back to another life, you will have to make all the right choices again.

It helps to know that we don't lose the spiritual qualities we have carefully sculpted over time. How do we remember what we knew in a previous life? Our intuition will guide us to make the right choices. You soul wants you to find out what direction to move in, where to put your time, and how to go about your life.

This is the reason why it is so important to work on your connection to the above through your intuition and through meditation, as to gain understanding into your own life and your life plan and so to determine what the best way is to move forward.

22. Be your own spiritual coach:
Open-up to discover your spiritual self.

Even though having a spiritual coach is in itself a positive thing, you still need to do the work yourself. You still need to know and find out much about yourself. In short, you still need to rely on yourself.

Why? Because it's your job, you bear the final responsibility for your life-show. It's important you give it your best shot.

For example, it is not always easy to precisely convey phenomena that are happening within us or communicate complex feelings that accompany such inner experiences.

When you do try to share something about an important past event, you can't expect yourself to accurately convey exactly what happened. Your memory will inevitably show flaws because you will be subjective and selective in your recollection of events.

Also, you will be limited to your capacity to verbalize what you experienced, and you are limited to language to describe often highly emotional situations. Even the language you speak matters, because one language might have a richer vocabulary than another.

The picture you will portray of any event or feeling to an outside person can never be as truthful as it is in your own mind. Next to that, there is the subjective interpretation of your information by the receiver, who has his or her own filters and limitations that affect, if not distort somewhat more, that what you communicate.

The quality of the larger environment in which you are called to restitute your experiences, also has an influence. Active listening skills, outside noise, emotional states, personal issues, and so on, all come into play when we communicate.

When we share something with our spiritual coach, we can do no more than rely on our best recollection of the facts, drawing from our best conscious memories. Meanwhile we must know that we convey only a part of the picture.

That's why it is important to trust one's own feelings and learn to trust one's own intuition, because they will serve you best in becoming your own spiritual coach or even therapist.

Take a lifelong friendship; you don't remember every little thing you have been through together, but your emotional intelligence actualizes every experience with any meaningful person and translates it into a feeling associated with that person, and this feeling is readily available, more readily available than all the memories. You see this when a smile appears on your face when you think of a loved one.

It follows, then, that we are ourselves, our own best witness and observer of our own life, and it could well be worthwhile to cultivate one's own abilities and intuition to interpret and construct meaning regarding the complex association between our physical envelope, our conscious and unconscious minds, our soul connection and the Divine.

It is impossible for anybody other than us to appreciate exactly the physical condition that we are in. Neither can we expect anybody else to exactly understand our life situations, our personal relationships, and other relevant life issues.

22. Be your own spiritual coach: Open-up to discover your spiritual self.

It is worth developing your own ability to listen to and analyze yourself and your situation, because, deep down, you know more than you can imagine. As this process is more about experiencing and feeling rather than knowing, an outside expert can only know and do so much.

We stand alone before this job anyway, it's the only real job we will ever have on this planet; managing ourselves through our own life to grow spiritually. Yes, much must be done alone. We come to this life alone and we will leave it the same way.

We cannot delegate the running of our own show. We can only grow spiritually if we are ready to think deeply about our life. We must embark upon the journey of thinking, investigating, reading, exchanging, contemplating, and meditating to advance slowly but surely on this path of spiritual growth.

The reward of acting in alignment with the very purpose of life, is that you are likely to encounter moments of bliss to show you that you are on the right track.

Of course, a spiritual coach can help to facilitate this process, but ultimately you have to do the job yourself. You are the one that has to change or grow.

You can start by defining what you find truly essential in your life, what you think is most important, most valuable, and most meaningful to you. In this way, you can finally concentrate on yourself and see how that resonates within.

When you've come up with some points, you can further ask yourself how you are doing with respect to these points, how you think you are coming along with your efforts, what you want to accomplish from here on, and how you want to do that.

To give your one and only real job in your life the best possible shot, you must be intrinsically motivated. As said before, that begins with the conscious thought or the intuitive realization that you are soul. You don't ever want to lose sight of this. It is the foundation upon which you build your spiritual understanding and knowledge.

Even though this point might be clear for you, you can still not be quite sure as to how to proceed from here. To straighten things out, you might want to talk to yourself to discuss your priorities in life and see where you're at with your spiritual progress. Call it an evaluation or a mid-term report if you want.

Go stand in front of the mirror, look yourself straight in the eye, and say:

"We need to talk. Yes, you and I."

23. Be your own spiritual coach:
Turn your inner voice into a precious ally.

In the last chapter I left off by saying that it can be beneficial to each one of us, to say to ourselves, when standing in front of the mirror, "we need to talk, yes, you and I."

At any age it is right to ask yourself for your life's progress report, but especially if you're in between thirty and sixty, it is a fine moment to do. All it takes to ask yourself that progress report, is to stand still and to look at yourself and ask, "How am I doing with my life?"

It is the right kind of question to ask yourself when you're forty for example. Because you might be halfway. At forty, you can still change some of the big lines in your life. You can still make career moves, restart a family, or simply change your own ways of doing or of being.

On the other hand, changes can be made at any time if one has the motivation. Thus, the question is pertinent at any age. It's never too soon, and it's never too late.

More important than age, one could argue, is maturity. Older people, who are generally more mature, have much to gain from reflecting on their lives and asking themselves what were the most interesting, the most challenging, and the most fulfilling experiences of their life.

How have these experiences influenced and shaped them as persons? And so on. Much can be collected when one puts him or herself in a comfortable countryside rocking chair and slip into retrospective mode.

You can't start early enough with your spiritual awakening and the cultivation of your natural interests in existential questions. It is never too late to wake up and to start with it, better late than never.

Some older people that really have used their time wisely and have gathered a wealth of spiritual knowledge and wisdom, might have found a way to share their findings with younger generations, and if they do, they carry out a high spiritual task or mission even.

When you ask yourself that tough question, "How am I doing with my life?," then you ask yourself, "How do you answer that question?"

Here's a technique that might help you, and you can't know if it will, unless you try. You speak the question out loud to yourself, and then listen to what you most naturally are inclined to respond.

Speak your mind freely, don't judge anything you hear yourself say, and see what you come up with. In this manner, you start an audible dialogue, not an inner discussion.

It's a way to "talk" that inner voice to the next level by giving 'him' the microphone. Instead of making all these little comments in the background, you point your finger at 'him' and ask 'him' to stand up and speak 'his' mind about your life.

It's like putting the inner discussion on a stage; it's still self-talk, but in a more responsible and hopefully constructive way. You are less likely to speak out loud all the little comments you speak so freely in the back of your mind, when you don't add your voice to it.

23. Be your own spiritual coach: Turn your inner voice into a precious ally.

When the inner voice stays small, it can become annoying at times, when it voices disapproval too easily, or when it becomes too greedy or too critical of people in general.

Speaking your mind out loud or externalizing the inner voice, obliges you to filter more, to discipline it, and make it more responsible. Most of us don't say all we think, when we speak we add a social touch to our thoughts; we become more nuanced. The idea is to make it more realistic, supportive, and constructive.

When you succeed in coming up with some interesting points, then you can shift to pep-talk to discuss what you can concretely make of it, to see where you can take it, and even verbalize a commitment of some sort to help you further in the direction you want to go.

You can negotiate and make a contract with yourself, by saying: "If you accomplish this and that, I'm ok to take 2 weeks of vacation this summer".

The trick is to change that inner voice from making little comments to a clear voice that can be a precious ally, friend or partner that helps to set you straight from time to time.

When I had difficult choices to make and couldn't make up my mind, I went to walk on the beach –but any natural setting or park would have been fine—, to have a serious talk with myself, and it helped me, so I wondered if it could work for other people too.

The walk for a talk proved to be a worthwhile technique for me. Driving back home, I had straightened out things with myself and set my priorities right.

Why did I do this? I did it to 'shake the tree', to question my ideas, to explain my thoughts, to be critical of my own opinions, and then to respond to my own criticism.

In the process, things cleared up. A consensus was reached, and a decision could be made with a commitment to seal it. I transformed the confusion into clarity, or so I told myself.

Even when I couldn't reach any kind of clear action to take, I knew I had tried to and that it wasn't possible this time. The wisest thing was to leave things roasting in my mind until the next time.

Most of the time, it wasn't an uphill battle. There were times when things were clear and nothing complicated needed to be treated or reviewed. As soon as I found I was done talking, I focused on the beach, the sand, the seawater, a seagull or anything else to break up the discussion.

This enabled me to enjoy the never-failing beauty of nature in a more relaxed mode. Each time I went for a talk with myself, I always opted for a beach that allowed me to walk for hours, not that I did so every time, but more so to guarantee my mind a large frame, a large setting to invite and facilitate out of the box ideas and creativity for my self-talk.

Next to the endlessness of the beach, I made sure to go there when there were only very few people around. Then when embarking upon the beach, I fired the following questions at myself, one at a time:

"How are things going?"

"How are you coming along with the set objectives?"

"Is there anything particular you're focusing on right now?"

23. Be your own spiritual coach: Turn your inner voice into a precious ally.

"Is there any problem that we need to see together?"

"Are you feeling ok with the way things are going?"

"Are there any choices you need to make?"

And so on.

These were typically the kind of questions I would ask myself, but asking these questions wasn't always necessary because I willingly started talking as soon as I started walking. It was like self-help, self-therapy, self-coaching and self-pep-talk even.

I always answered honestly, I was alone with myself, nobody around anyway, I could speak my mind. Sometimes I would answer when asked if I was happy with my efforts:

"It's ok, I'm doing what I need to do, but I could do more, I could do better. You know me, I'm easily distracted, but I'll try to do more. I'll try to do better."

The goal of the walk-talk exercise was first of all to question my own wants and needs, which was the most complicated part because it required self-knowledge. I wasn't easy on myself and fired all kinds of questions to test my motivation.

In college I had a double major, International Studies and Psychology and I remember a discussion on the beach about the choice of a specific elective course: human biology. I learned that day, that besides an arguable connection to psychology, I had some unfinished business with human biology, since I had not given my best shot to biochemistry in high-school and wanted a rematch. In high-school I had found the subject matter interesting but lacked sufficient motivation and discipline to study seriously.

This example shows us that through this type of discussion one can find out hidden motivations; something less obvious for you to come up with when merely scanning the surface with your conscious mind.

In the process, my wants and needs were adjusted to the possibilities that my environment had to offer and so, conscious decisions could be taken.

If you try this self-talk technique, chances are it will work for you because we are all uniquely capable of developing our own creative edge that will make the dialogue function.

Self-talk takes yet unclear 'subjects' out of the background and brings them to full awareness, by putting them in the spotlight, where they can be looked at, talked about, and in that process, clarified.

By making things as clear as possible, we limit eventual regrets that might pop up later on if things don't turn out right, in the immediate future.

The point is that it felt good to talk freely and openly about everything. It got the communication flowing, and sometimes I was surprised what that inner dialogue could bring me in terms of new ideas or even solutions. It's like opening the tap, letting it flow, and starting a psycho-spiritual creative process, much like brainstorming out loud.

Think about it, if you will, and then try to see if it could do you any good.

24. Be your own spiritual coach:
Spend your precious time wisely.

In the previous chapter, I "talked" about self-talk and how we can try to let the inner voice speak out to make it more of a mature partner in our growth process.

Another point of the inner voice is to try to keep the dialogue focused on the purpose of your life, the one thing we shouldn't take lightly. I wish for nobody to say to himself or herself one day that he or she simply never gave it any thought while realizing that one should have.

This is a much greater problem than many of us might think, for the simple reason that our life(time) passes much quicker than we imagine when we are young. Many people do run into this type of realization, and that is truly a sad thing.

Be honest with yourself and prepare tough questions to ask and to answer because it's all about you. This is serious business, more serious than whatever other business there is.

This is your life, for you to succeed, and it is in your own hands. You have to make it happen with what you've got, and be assured, you have what it takes, always. In any situation of your life, you stand perfectly equipped to do the job at hand.

The question is to figure out what exactly your job is, because no two persons have the same job in life. We all have different karmic backgrounds, with generally both positive and negative karma, so we have different lessons to learn and different things that we will find on our path.

We all have a different life plan, a different road map, but although our individual ways can differ enormously, we're all headed in the same direction.

Whatever your job is, be confident that you're right for the job. You were made to play the part you're playing. You are uniquely fit for this role, to be the hero of your life, and nobody can play that part for you. Nobody can do a better job than you.

If you think you are carrying a heavy load, it might be so, but your load is in proportion to what you can handle or at least, what you must sail through, what you must experience. Trust this principle.

Be ambitious in your statements of that what you want to reach and put your qualities there where other people can benefit from them too, and not only yourself or your family.

Do not only focus on making money, for the best in life money can't buy, but focus on where your qualities have the greatest positive impact.

Have high hopes for yourself. Be positive. Commit yourself to do what you need to do to make it happen, to succeed in your life. Then review it in the afterlife with your old buddies with a smile on your astral face.

If you're not completely happy with how things are going for you, tell yourself that you didn't come here just to be happy but rather to do a good job. The better you do your job, the more likely you are to see happiness coming your way.

I most wish you spiritual growth.

25. Be your own spiritual coach:
Bring positive energy, create beauty and change the world.

When analyzing your life, and thinking where to put your time and attention from now on, consider the following:

The best way to work for a better future for yourself is to adopt an approach that includes other people in your nice plans and direct at least some of your efforts to either help or make other people feel better, or even happy if you can.

I take it that the contribution we make to other people is seen in the light of the means we have and the efforts we make. One can simply transfer knowledge, teach, or explain. One can help other people who are less able, and so contribute greatly.

Doing something for somebody else makes somebody else happy, and the giving makes you happy too, and all you give will be given back to you in one way or another. We create a positive flow or movement of energy and it can be contagious. If so, good for you.

It functions much like a boomerang. The type of energy you send out into your world, good or bad, might fly away and disappear out of sight, but one day, it will certainly come back to offer you the same.

The key in your life is to be able to create beauty. Real beauty, in a spiritual sense, is what is uplifting and beneficial to a greater group.

When you're well in your adult life, the beauty you can make is to be discovered in the specific life situations and relationships that you actually have in your life. When we create beauty, we impact other people positively, and take their 'spirits' to a higher level, for a moment or forever.

How can you go about "creating beauty"? In our every day life, being nice and gentle to people will do the job, but If you want to be a spiritual 'warrior', you might take your smile and gentle touch into the social arena, and 'testcase' your empathy and kindness to see if they have the power to transform.

In alignment with the higher forces, you might indeed have the power to transform, to disarm, to turnaround deadlocked situations, to re-unite, to resolve unfinished business and even much more, if it needs to be so. Never forget that it is our actions that make or break us, and not the end result, because we have no power over it. Initiate a flow of positive energy and see how it will lift you up while you're doing it.

Look specifically to develop your own qualities and abilities to understand other people, to be kind and compassionate. Ask yourself what you could do to be an even greater positive presence in the lives of the people around you.

Still, whatever your situation is, you can always create beauty; even when you're in a very difficult situation, there is always a way to create beauty. If you aren't sure, let yourself be inspired, ask for help, or meditate on it and see what comes.

You can be an under-performer in your job, you can even have failed professionally several times, and still succeed beautifully your life-job, if you know how to walk in alignment with the higher forces.

25. Be your own spiritual coach: Bring positive energy, create beauty and change the world.

If you can act according to high principles, you will, sooner or later, create beauty, and it is that beauty that you were able to make through your never-failing efforts that will set you apart in the eyes of the maker. It will make the world a better place and it will make your soul shine, bringing you peace, joy, and bliss.

I wish you all a most fruitful spiritual journey.

26. How to start up your spiritual practice?

If you want to move forward on your spiritual path, here are some points to consider:

1. Make room for spiritual practice in your schedule.

It all begins with making some time available, start by taking 20 minutes for the total experience. This includes many of the next steps discussed below and doesn't mean you have to sit perfectly still, meditating for 20 minutes.

Do try to commit yourself to at least two or three sessions per week, of each no less than 20 minutes.

2. External environment: try to find a quiet place.

You need a quiet place where you will be sure you will not be disturbed and where you will have little risk of being distracted by loud noises, voices, traffic, and so on.

Even a tiny room is fine, you only need a place to sit still.

3. Cut yourself off from as much interference as you can.

It is especially important to turn off your smartphone and to leave it in another room or at least out of sight.

26. How to start up your spiritual practice?

If you simply turn it off, you still know in the back of your mind that your phone is within reach, and that knowledge might come to distract you when you are trying to think of nothing.

4. Put on comfortable clothes and find a comfortable position.

Before starting, put on comfortable clothes. It is important not to feel bothered by a tight belt, a tie, your shoes, or anything exerting pressure on your body. Anything at all that feels uncomfortable must be attended to because if not, it will keep distracting you, begging your attention, and keeping you earthbound, vividly linked to the physical body.

When you do have things in place and under control, you can start to sit upright, with or without a backrest. Then, close your eyes, then try not to think of anything else; just let yourself be and appreciate that moment of calmness.

Take on a comfortable position and then try to sit perfectly still and see how long you succeed in not moving.

At the end of your session, it is worthwhile to be attentive if there are body parts that start to ache after a while because once you know, you can figure out a better physical posture for your next session. Try to accommodate yourself as to adjust all the time until you have found your ideal position to meditate in.

5. Arrange the lights as to suit your personal preference.

I prefer to meditate in a dimly lit room, because I don't want that surplus of artificial light unnecessarily stimulating my brain, while sitting with my eyes closed, trying to relax. You may want to experiment with different lighting as to see what suits you best.

6. Increase the duration of your spiritual session gradually.

First do 20 minutes, then 25 minutes, then 30 minutes, and so on. Do what comes naturally and what feels comfortable, no need to force yourself into sitting any longer than you feel like. Over time you will discover what duration works best for you in the beginning, and then allow it to evolve.

7. Internal environment: putting yourself in the right mindset.

Leave the outside material world behind, forget it exists even. I slowly close a heavy door and then speak to myself: "... and now by closing this door, I shut myself off from the outside world." (Of course, any door will do the job).

The idea is that your meditation practice is held in a little world of its own. It can be tiny, but it should shut you off from noise and movement.

Try to empty your mind as much as you can. Try to think of nothing. Try to sit perfectly still and see how long you succeed in not moving.

With time you will increase your meditation skills and learn to sit perfectly still and long enough not to feel your body anymore, and so, making your meditation session a more profound experience.

26. How to start up your spiritual practice?

8. Try to make it a daily thing, then slowly it will become the "main event" of your day.

It is important to be a regular practitioner because all learning needs repetition. If the interval between your sessions is too great, you will have to get back into the "groove" each time. It's easier to build and maintain that continuous energy with shorter experiences that follow up on one another.

By being constant in your practice, you strengthen the process that you set for yourself.

9. Try to be in any close-by natural setting whenever you can; a city park, a river, a lake, a field, and enjoy the scenery all around you.

These are moments of contemplation when we're halfway between our regular life and meditation; we are still in the physical world, but we sit motionless for a long while and stare at things from a more peripheral position, somewhat apart or even isolated.

In these moments, we are not looking for small talk with strangers. We keep to ourselves and obviously avoid crowded places.

When you succeed in having the external conditions just about right, and manage to leave your earthly matters to rest in your mind, you might start to contemplate why you are here or what to do with your life from here on.

If you have no specific spiritual topics or existential questions to contemplate, then please sit still and 'see' what might manifest.

10. Once in a while, visit, if possible, a more impressive natural site.

Go high in the mountains, go sit on the shore of a big lake, walk on the high cliffs on rough coasts, or seek out any other equally impressive panoramic viewpoint that offers a privileged position to admire the beauty of creation and our own littleness in it.

These are the places or sites we sit in awe, impressed by the vastness and grandeur of nature. Here we stand small as humans before the grandeur of nature.

Here, if we can isolate ourselves on a rock by a lake, on a mountain top, on a deserted beach, or wherever possible, you can take more time to admire the beauty and let yourself be inspired and meditate deeply if conditions allow.

It is important to give yourself moments of tranquil contemplation on the bigger picture, and all that transcends our little earthly and sometimes even short life.

11. Address yourself to the Highest, and use prayer as an introduction.

If you feel like it, pray to our Heavenly Father, to our Divine Mother, to the Universe, or to the Source. Whatever suits you most. For people that don't believe there is a Heavenly Father, there is a spirit world out there that does receive our prayers.

12. Start a group with like-minded practitioners.

You might think about starting a group with like-minded spiritual people to discuss one's progress as well as other topics of spiritual or existential nature.

13. Keep a journal.

Keep a journal or a notebook to write down significant events. It might be interesting to write down your progress; a little note recapping each session will do.

Sometimes there are spiritual issues or questions that come to mind when practicing that you may forget later. When you keep a notebook readily available, you can jot them down for later review alone or to share them with your fellow practitioners.

You may also note something that struck you as strange or coincidental, or simply noteworthy, in retrospect you might discover it was a synchronicity, or a meaningful coincidence.

In this way, we grow in understanding, our mental map of the world expands and becomes more accurate. Meanwhile, we cultivate our sense of seeing through the superficial layer of life.

14. Sign up for a spiritual retreat.

If you are doing all the above, then you are already engaged in your spiritual practice, but next to the above, and with time, one might think about a spiritual retreat in a natural site for a weekend, a week, or longer.

This can be to meditate, practice mindfulness, observe silence and stick to it, or anything of the kind.

15. Sign up for a spiritual group workshop.

As opposed to a retreat where you often spend time alone, in meditation, in contemplation, in stillness and the like, you can also do groupwork where people create together in the right energy of mutual positive regard.

I believe when people experiment with long meditation sessions of several hours too early in their spiritual practice, they might experience frustration which could prove difficult to overcome.

People are likely to run into their own pressing issues and problems time and again, because not everything can be easily brushed away, parked out of sight, or put in just perspective when we are starting on this path.

I believe in the good of group interaction because, although we are all unique and have our own issues and problems, we are all incarnates struggling with comparable issues and problems. We can learn from one another. We can support one another. We can give our honest opinion if presented respectfully. We can voice constructive criticism, and we can give positive feedback.

Next to that, the emotional aspect is much stronger when you do group work, as compared to when you spend more time alone. When we are not yet perfectly in place from a psychological and spiritual point of view, we still need to voice what we feel and experience inside and engage in active communication to discuss it.

26. How to start up your spiritual practice?

You can do group-work where all group-members can comment and then balance it with individual sessions to check upon each individual person.

Some have more difficulty functioning in a group than others and almost disappear into the background, while they might show very talkative in a one-on-one setting.

Individual sessions are especially good to mix with group work, as they allow you to verify that all is going well for each and every person in a secure setting.

For any of us, to be lastingly productive, we all need to feel at our place, listened to and appreciated. For us to aboard personal and/or sensitive issues we need to be met with unconditional positive regard.

Spiritual group-work serves the purpose of sharing where you are in your spiritual development. It provides an opportunity to exchange with others on the experience of spiritual progress and raising one's consciousness.

This process can have a therapeutic effect when we try to see our personal issues and problems –that are often part of the spiritual journey–, in a spiritual light. Learning to express to others our suffering, may help to make it more bearable.

The take-away can be to see what things you could focus on in the future, how you could best continue in your life, aiming for more spiritual growth.

16. Open up to your intuition; learn to trust it.

When you do your meditation for some time, it might also start to influence the quality of your being and inner psychology while not meditating. You may become more aware of your environment and generally calmer.

By sitting motionless and turning your attention inward, you train yourself to listen and to be aware of anything happening around you. If you sit still long enough, you might find that things come to mind.

In calmness, we "perceive" things better; we feel, hear, and see things more accurately, more precisely, and this state can help us be more intuitive.

27. Considerations to take along on the spiritual path.

I doubt any person engaged on the spiritual path would find that the lion's share of people's desires, wants and needs, is spiritually sound or justified to strive for.

Why do I say "spiritually sound or justified"?, because from an earthly point of view all people's desires are explainable, understandable, and thus, they seem justified.

The problem is that the pursuit of earthly objectives might not get us very far in the heavens, if, from a spiritual point of view, these objectives manifest predominantly ego related motivations and lack considerations for the common good.

We believe when we work hard, we are doing a good job, but it is less obvious that all our earthly efforts and enterprises will be automatically validated when put in the light of our spiritual evolution. If your efforts and projects are purely ego-driven, and no contribution to spiritual growth is likely to be had in the process, your enterprise is unlikely to yield excitement here above.

Put your desires, wants and needs to the test, try to see them in a spiritual light, and see how many of them melt away. Please think carefully about the kind of a wish-list you identify with, because all our choices have consequences. If you include other people in your nice plans, and try to serve a higher purpose, you will be followed with much interest.

When we put our desires, wants and needs in a spiritual light, it takes all the inequality between people and their material conditions away, because on a spiritual level we are all soul. Our soul is neither male nor female, neither black nor white, and neither rich nor poor.

Wve are soul before we're born, and when we die, we leave our physical envelope with Mother Earth and rise to our Heavenly Father –the universe, the source—, where we continue our journey once again, as a soul.

Our physical life on this planet is given to us to learn something, to contribute to something, to accomplish something, and this is equally accessible or doable for all.

Why are we all equally fit to do this job?

We all have a unique heritage. We all are unique souls, and we all are unique human beings. This makes for unique life-plans, and so each of us has a unique job to do.

How to tackle our life job?

Focus on yourself and do what you must, do what is noble. Never lose sight of what is essential to bear in mind: you are a soul. Don't lose too much time with (social) trivialities, but stay focused on the main event of your life; spiritual progress.

Also, it is on earth that man discriminates against his fellow man. The one that does so is small and ignorant, but every wrongful action is recorded, creating negative karma.

27. Considerations to take along on the spiritual path.

Even when wronged, try not to keep any hard feelings; trust that underlying spiritual principles govern our world and that all accounts must and will be balanced in due time.

In life, we're often too close up on things, too emotionally involved, and at times, all seems wrong, but when we cultivate a higher understanding of life and step back to look at things from afar, things may fall into place, and we can start to make sense of it.

Life is not a material race or a competition of social situations. You only need yourself and no other fancy equipment to succeed.

How do you succeed in your life?

Do your best with all that you find on your plate. Don't get too impressed and distracted by the material illusion.

One could argue that the king and the pauper could well have similar life experiences in all core areas of their earthly existence, although the physical setting, the theater, will differ immensely.

Differences in comfort levels or social situations can't have a decisive bearing on the net result of one's life because both rich and poor are most touched and affected by health, love, family relations, friendships, and so on, since these subjects touch us equally, irrespective of social class or personal wealth.

The essence of our life experience is to be found in all the things that money can't touch, that money can't control, that money can't make, and that money can't buy.

If we want to grow spiritually, we cannot limit our perspective and understanding to earthly life, not even while living. Finding out what the right way to live is, begins with constructing one's understanding of life. We can greatly enhance our understanding of life, when we learn about what awaits us in the afterlife.

I was drawn to investigate about death in my mid-twenties, it helped me to construct clear ideas about the afterlife, and since then, my concept of death served me well throughout my life. I learned that my concept of death is the same as the concept of life, because in our spiritual evolution, life on earth and afterlife in the other dimension, simply follow up on one another, they are part of a process, much like night and day. The process is ever revolving until all that has to be acquired and let go off is accomplished, and reunification with the divine has been reached.

So we see the success (or 'failure') of a lifetime, as seen from the highest perspective, is not primarily related to, neither depended on, nor limited by material conditions.

In the end, the power of material possessions that we may enjoy in the physical world is also limited to the physical world; its reach doesn't extent beyond physical life. When life ceases, its functionality stops too. In the heavens 'we' do not appreciate likewise material wealth and social status as we do here below.

It is good to bear in mind for people who see themselves as having modest conditions, that money, although it can upgrade one's environment, it cannot impact, change or determine the essence of what our life experience is all about, because that is left for each and every one of us to accomplish, with our own free will. In the end, we are all equally well-equipped.

27. Considerations to take along on the spiritual path.

So, never belittle yourself because you think you're not a 'big shot' in this crazy world, but rather give your life your 'best shot', no matter what your circumstances are.

All the power you need in your life is right there, in your mind, you just have to inject it into your actions, and when you can do that, ... you become the hero of your life. Go for it!

I wish you well.

www.ingramcontent.com/pod-product-compliance
Lightning Source LLC
LaVergne TN
LVHW092007090526
838202LV00001B/43